Sell & Resell Your Magazine Articles

Gordon Burgett

WRITER'S DIGEST BOOKS
CINCINNATI, OHIO

This hardcover edition of *Sell and Resell Your Magazine Articles* features a "self-jacket" that eliminates the need for a separate dust jacket. It provides sturdy protection for your book while it saves paper, trees and energy.

Other fine Writer's Digest Books are available from your local bookstore or direct from the publisher.

01 00 99 98 97   5 4 3 2 1

Library of Congress Cataloging-in-Publication Data

Burgett, Gordon.
    Sell and resell your magazine articles / by Gordon Burgett.
        p.   cm.
    Includes index.
    ISBN 0-89879-799-3 (alk. paper)
    1. Journalism—Authorship—Marketing 2. Feature writing—Marketing I. Title
PN161.B8245 1997
070.5′2′0973—dc21   97-15359
                                                                         CIP

Edited by Jack Heffron and Roseann Biederman
Cover design by Stephanie Redman

ACKNOWLEDGMENTS

I wish to thank at least 700 editors who encouraged me by buying the promise of my words, then keeping me sufficiently honest, clear and informative to get them on their published pages. If it weren't for them, this book wouldn't exist. I'd probably be a cheese salesman or a spy instead.

And to Writer's Digest Books, who accepted my very first book proposal (which I then rejected) seventeen years ago, for asking again. This acceptance is due in no small part to Mert Ransdell, who has kept me gratefully in the neighborhood by including almost all of my writing books in the Writer's Digest Book Club; Bill Brohaugh, a friend who kept a book idea alive; Jack Heffron, who posed and framed the idea then gave me free reign; and Roseann Biederman, who pulled the parts together with the deftest of hands. Thanks also to Dan Carlinsky, ASJA, who helped me weave through the labyrinth of electronic rights. If I goofed on anything in this book, it's despite their best efforts!

Finally, to those who hear me speak about writing, who keep the joy of the process alive and for my staff at my own publishing company who suffered with love my disappearances "to write a book": Linda Lange, Trish Cardwell, Sharon Garrett, and Wally Lange.

ABOUT THE AUTHOR

Gordon Burgett has published numerous books of nonfiction and more than 1,600 newspaper and magazine articles. Three of his books—*The Travel Writer's Guide*, *The Writer's Guide to Query and Cover Letters*, and *How to Sell More Than 75% of Your Writing*—have been Writer's Digest Book Club selections. He has produced twenty-six instructional audiocassettes and appears regularly at writer's conferences throughout the country. He lives in Santa Maria, California.

DEDICATION

This book is for Marsha Freeman, who is also Marsha Burgett. A sweetheart.

TABLE OF CONTENTS

INTRODUCTION

Putting your ideas and knowledge in print to share with others and getting rewarded for it is what this book is all about.

There are a hundred ways not to sell articles or books to editors who are eager to buy and able to pay. And several approaches that work very well. In this book we'll focus on the latter: the how and why of putting your copy profitably and reliably in print.

Two things are crucial to doing that: a solid idea at the core of your writing and solid writing to develop that core. Still, the best writer in captivity can remain unpublished for want of a sprinkle of knowledge about how to sell.

Selling is part of writing, unless it's being done solely for therapy or the writer owns the press. Still, the writer's focus should never be on the selling, per se, but rather on the proper fit of ideas and words to the needs of a reading public. The selling is a proper matching, to put your gilded phrases before those needing that form and type of gold.

Two elements you don't often find linked with the simple selling process will also find their way to these pages.

The first is a strong emphasis on converting the idea being sold into more sales, not only by reselling to similar markets, but by expanding the research and "topic-spoking" it far more extensively. It's how you expand a $350 one-article idea into a $3,500 mini-winner or a $35,000 jackpot.

The second element takes that thought even further. It says that the articulation and word mastery central to writing success is not dissimilar to success in other media, such as speeches, seminars, audio- or videocassettes and more.

A last thought. I'm struck by both how little things have changed since I wrote my first "writing book" in 1981 and by how much the tools and means differ.

The way you sell to editors today is the way I sold in high school, college and every stage since. I haven't failed to change. The needs are essentially the same, and the ways the editors meet them are likewise the same.

But computers were as unheard of as my earlier scenario, where salesfolk fanned and fed writers. Fax was facts misspelled. E-mail was mail filed under the letter *E*. Sending a book by disk was done in science fiction. And to modemize copy had an erotic tone to it, which probably meant sending it in a plain brown wrapper.

Is this more than you wanted to read about? Does it sound a bit overwhelming? The primary focus is getting those first words in print and paid for, then repeating it until you're looking for more outlets that likewise pay and need your knowledge. You can use the process described as narrowly or as fully as you wish, moving up the income and time-involvement scales when you are ready. Better to show you the full path and put you in control of your own distance and destiny than limit the scope of these pages because some might be intimidated.

So let's get to it. This system works if you use it. Try it. We need to read what you know.

Part One

BEGIN WITH THE SALE IN MIND

CHAPTER ONE

Some Practical Considerations Before You Get Started

So you want to sell your writing! Great! Many, many thousands do it, some just once, some now and then and some repeatedly to pay the food and rent. Some even get rich by selling their words. Welcome to the writing community.

The outlook for writers

How many of us are there? In 1995 there were 12,537 magazines in the U.S. alone. If each averaged ten articles, that was 125,370 articles. If we balanced the newcomers against the heavily selling professionals and they averaged six sales apiece, that would mean almost 21,000 writers are keeping those pages filled. Yet the official numbers read differently. According to the *Occupational Outlook Handbook* of the Bureau of Labor Statistics (Spring 1996), there are 272,000 writers and editors in the U.S.

Where are the rest of those writers hiding? I'd suggest that some may be doing just that—calling themselves writers but either not writing or not selling. Others may be providing finished copy for the radio or TV, movies, newsletters, Internet, ad sheets, junk mail and bulletin boards.

Then there's the huge book market. According to Dan Poynter, author of *The Self-Publishing Manual* (Para Publications), who based his findings on the *Books in Print* CD-ROM, 119,000 new titles saw light in 1995 (of which about 5,000 were reprints). There were 53,000 publishers in 1995, plus those who didn't release a book that year or who did but did not use an ISBN (International Standard Book Number). Of the 53,000, the large, easily recognized major houses numbered 23 (15 in New York City); about 300 were medium-sized houses (like Writer's Digest Books); and the 52,500+ were small houses. The number increased 11,500 from 1994, though it has usually increased about 8,000 new publishers annually in the past few years. The most astounding number: There were 1,063,000 books in print in 1995.

Clarifying your goals

With the staggering number of potential markets for your work, there's no reason to ask why you want to sell your writing. Hats off to you! You've just taken a very important step, by declaring that you want to sell your writing. Your have clearly stated your goal and outlined your terms.

But you've also provoked some questions:

- To whom do you want to sell your writing? To which editor(s) of which publication(s)?
- How often do you want to sell that writing? Once? Monthly? Regularly?
- How much do you want to earn? Will anything be gratefully accepted? An extra $100 a month? Enough to lead a comfortable life? Or enough to amass a fortune?
- How soon do you want to be in print?
- Which kind of writing do you want to sell? What's it about? Or just anything that escapes your pen?

You hadn't expected so many questions? All you wanted to do was get inspired, write in the glow of that enlightenment, let your hand serve as the medium for genius in flow, run the resulting prose through spell-check, and zip it off to the highest paying publication, money due in thirty days?

That's precisely the formula of most wanna-be writers, the kind often referred to in the trade as oral writers. They talk great articles, eye-bulging books and TV scripts that would be bought sight unseen. Good thing too, being bought sight unseen, because the only thing oral writers don't do is write. That's the only missing ingredient to their cornering the market in a writing medium.

For the rest of us, the dream, plan or compulsion to sell our writing must be filtered through a sieve of selling reality. That doesn't make the words less lovely or inspired or needed, it simply puts them into a mind-set, time frame, action plan and order that makes them buyable.

The crux of the mind-set is your getting into the mind of the buyers, the editors to whom you want to sell your copy. How do they think, what do they want to buy, how do they want to be approached and what must you do to get your idea and a possible article moved to the top of their buy lists? That is the thrust of the next chapter.

The time frame isn't one uniform schedule of what you do on what date. Magazine articles have four crucial time moments as they pertain to you: when the editor receives the query, when he responds, when you submit the finished article and when the editor sends you the final reply. Newspaper editors have three different time pegs: when you submit the copy with a cover note, when you send the photos (if requested) and when the piece sees light in print. It also varies for book editors, reprint buyers and purchasers in other media. Those will all be explained as the processes themselves are revealed.

The action plan starts and ends with you. It is built around the steps you must take to sell, research, write, edit and submit your copy—then sell it again and again. Writing is an integral part of the action plan—researching and writing with a singular purpose: the creation of a selling article or book. That comes after you have the necessary details: what the editor wants to buy, what you can write, what of the material gathered is used to create the final copy and how and when the editor wants it submitted. Most of this book centers on your action plan, each as varied as the article at hand yet all consistent with a general selling/writing pattern that has scarcely changed in the past three decades.

Order is what makes it all happen. A selling, then writing order—in that order. The words in an order that makes the topic and the writing jump from the page and shout, properly, that this work comes from the mind and pen of a professional. The shout that makes editors beam with delight. (Yes, editors do beam with delight. Some of them. More important, a proper shout that gets them to pay on time!)

What do editors want?

Editors have one goal that overrides all others: to fill their pages with copy and artwork so good that it will leave the reader begging for more (and, where appropriate, asking to renew and extend their subscriptions). To achieve this, they look for tight, well-crafted, accurate articles that fill their peculiar needs.

Not all of those pages are filled with the kind of text you sell. Many contain the advertising, which indirectly pays your check. Some include titles, the masthead, public service announcements and flat-out fillers. So the number of column inches or pages available for your material is limited. Some of that is even filled by staff-written items, regular columns and sometimes guest slots. Not much room for rambling, pointless, endless prose.

Rather, every article bought fills a clearly defined purpose. It occupies 1,000 or 1,750 or 2,500 words of space (the editor equates those to picas) in which to inform, inspire, anger, instruct, harangue, amuse or do whatever it is you propose. If artwork is included—usually photography, charts, maps, line drawings or graphs—you must further deduct the space that occupies from the word space you provide. Rambling is out.

A good way to view the editor's role and yours is to put yourself in the editor's shoes and mind, then try to figure out where both of your best interests overlap. The "win-win" analogy is overused, but it couldn't be more appropriate than here. Those areas where both of you emerge victorious by helping each other are the starting blocks of a mutually long and beneficial relationship.

You say you don't want a long relationship with an editor, you just want the old skinflint to buy one article so you can quickly end your writing career? Fine. You must still find a place where both of you win by having those precious words on that editor's page.

Just who are these editors anyway?

Surprisingly, they look and even think like us. About half are men, the other half women. Their median age is probably 35–45, with some in their 20s and a few still roaring at 70. They are probably college graduates with some newspaper-writing experience. They are most likely articulate and a tad cynical. Most also have (or had) a spouse, plus children, car payments, nagging pains, resident guilt and the sense that life is whizzing by too quickly for them to realize their dreams, however precise or vague. They are a lot like us: They take pride in what they're doing; they are responsible; they want to be judged by their performance and they know they are underpaid.

Where do your interests and theirs overlap? They need sharp ideas unveiled through scintillating copy that is irresistible to their readers. You need a place to print your copy that will pay you well for your effort and artistic skill.

Your common meeting ground is that publishing hole on their pages.

Editors are constantly seeking reliable, prompt, skilled writers who can provide good ideas and even better text. Their stables are never too full.

They encounter writers many different ways. Those already on staff. Some they knew at earlier jobs. One or two might be related. Some are interns spending part of their senior college year in the publishing office. Everybody they meet at cocktail parties has a book or script half done. And many total strangers, who audaciously mail them one-page letters called queries in which they propose to write a full article about the topic briefly described.

You are in that last category. Of all those listed, you are best positioned for prompt and serious consideration, thanks to the query letter. Queries are the key needed to enter the "win-win" zone. The rest will also have to submit query letters so the editor can read precisely what they want to write about and see how they write. Anything else is talk, the special domain of oral (read nonselling) writers.

The all-important query letter

So, the key to the gate of serious contention is the query letter. (This differs for simultaneous submissions, such as newspapers or reprints, as we'll see later. The key there is the submission of a final manuscript.) What in a query opens the gate? Why would an editor, whom you do not know, agree to read your manuscript, use it and pay you, based on a one-page letter? Chapter six, appropriately the longest chapter in this book, defines queries and replies to this question in loving detail. A summary here gives the highlights.

A query letter sells an article idea and shows, in the writing, that you are the person who should prepare that article for that editor. Queries explain what you want to write about, why those particular readers would be interested (if it isn't obvious), any expertise you bring to the subject—or the experts you will cite (if needed)—any sidebars or artwork you can provide and your writing/publishing background.

The editor operates from a specific mind-set. She has readers who buy or subscribe to the publication to read about certain topics. If the magazine contains motorcycling in its title, nothing on its pages veers far from motorcycling. Running magazines talk about the hundred facets of running. Even seemingly omnibus gender magazines are gender biased and have a clearly defined buyer profile that determines the boundaries of its readers' interests, by such things as age, educational level, residence, financial status and employment.

So you too are bound by that mind-set. Not that you can't propose an article about guerrilla warfare to the *Journal of Swiss Cuisine*; you can. The editor might enjoy your query, laughing heartily and sharing it with friends, but that article will never appear in that magazine. The topic throws you out of the win-win zone. If that editor prints your article on those pages, the editor loses.

Thus your success in querying starts with a subject wanted by the editor for her pages. Then the editor must get a sense from the limited writing at hand that you can produce accurate copy, well written and delivered on time. The experts cited and your background will strengthen that sense. The actual writing in the query—spelling, grammar, facility of expression, length of sentences, clarity, logic, order and the flow and ease of reading—all show at once that the end product will be at least above the minimal level of writing needed to appear in print on that editor's pages.

The editor rejects those queries that are clearly unusable. Those not rejected will be noted on the production calendar several months off, by title and author's name. Then the editor responds to each person listed indicating an interest in buying the manuscript on speculation and sometimes adds specific stipulations, such as the submission deadline, a different angle to consider, word length and/or pay rate.

The final step is your research, writing and submission of the copy by the deadline date.

The article appears, you get paid, you and the editor are pleased and the elements needed for similar sales in the future have been planted.

For you to create a writing career, or at least get into print at the outset, you must somehow get that editor's attention. That is done by suggesting a needed topic and an angle that ties it to the readership. Then by showing the editor, through that same query, that you can follow through promptly and reliably.

What you are saying by implication in the query is that you have an idea you think her readers would like to know more about, and that if the editor gives you a "go-ahead," a positive reply on speculation, you can form-fit the article to the readers' interests and needs while keeping the text within the stylistic and content limitations of the publication. In other words, once you get the nod, the article will fit the readers like a glove.

Don't editors differ? Will this one-size-fits-all querying key to print success work without fail?

Of course not. Some editors don't want to be queried. Some editors say yes to everybody, then reject virtually every finished manuscript submitted. Some editors receive the query, then retire or expire and it disappears. Some editors will direct you to approach the topic this way, then ask you later where the weird slant came from. Who promised that editors would all be alike?

But what has been suggested will work for 95 percent of the editors, and God knows what will work with the rest—and who cares? Focus on that win-win zone and the need to fill a page hole with first-rate copy, and selling your writing can lead to an exciting, profitable career.

Building relationships with editors

A last point: career. You may have another career, or several, well launched, and writing is simply an adjunct activity that reinforces what you really do for fun or money. Fine. Best wishes in whatever you pursue. But if you don't address each sale like it is the bedrock of a coming career, you considerably diminish the chances of that sale and you further reduce any hopes of any writing career should you change your mind later.

Consider every contact with any editor, however jerky or suspect, as a crucial step in a career ladder. Wow that editor with a masterful query. Create the best manuscript possible. Provide anything else the editor needs to make that article shine. Then return with another powerful query and repeat the same winning steps with the subsequent articles.

The benefits?

That editor gets progressively more eager to include and keep you in the fold. Queries are responded to quicker and more fully. Your pay rate increases. After a couple of sales, most editors begin making assignments (with a kill fee possible) rather than buying on speculation. And when an idea occurs, it will be to you that the editor will turn, calling or writing you to discuss your producing copy for those pages!

Moreover, editors move around. When they move, you have an inside route into that new publication. So do their associate editors, and they too, familiar with your work with the original editor, will often contact you as they rise to the top spot.

Editors also have friends. At conferences, conventions, quick lunches or on the phone, the names of key writers who are proven reliable and gifted get bandied about. This makes future queries better received. It also leads to telephone calls asking you to query.

Sadly, it also works in reverse. Stiff an editor and you get a free listing on his no-buy list kept in the middle drawer, which is shared with the associate and assistant editors. Burn him badly enough and the whole informal network will know.

You see, editors are just like us: humans who have a job to do and respond to others in direct proportion to how much they help them do that job well.

Timing

Before you design a selling program to magazines, newspapers or book publishers—or any combination thereof—you must answer the timing questions first. These key questions should be answered early on.

1. *When* do you want to be in print?
2. *How often*? Once? Now and then? Five times a week? Regularly for the rest of your life?
3. *When* do editors buy the kind of material you want to write and sell? (If never, do not pass go. As Mark Twain said, "If you

want to make a living by writing poetry, first learn to chop wood." If they never buy poetry, start chopping.)

If you want to be in print immediately, or very soon, you must pursue a different path than those whose time frames are more elastic, longer and less frantic. To get in print quickly, write for newsletters, newspapers and newscasts. Or paste free copy on walls or Net screens.

If you want to be in print soon, magazines should be added to the list. A few are dailies, others weeklies, most monthlies. The less frequently they publish, the longer your copy waits. For a monthly, most magazines take two months (sometimes three) to take form.

If time is even less important, books take longest. You can crank out a self-published tome in a month or two after the camera-ready copy and cover reach the printer. Most major houses take from twelve to eighteen months to produce the final book from final draft copy.

How often do you want to be in print? If it's just once, so you can notch that belt and move on to something less sedentary, there's no particular hurry. Get to it when you're ready, dig deeply and make your solo printing memorable. (Beware, though. Once you're in print, it's hard not to do it again, particularly if you move on to success in other fields.)

But if you want to be in print widely, often and soon, learn the process that begins in the next chapter, get comfortable selling to the various formats (newspapers, magazines and perhaps books), then focus on the chapter about topic-spoking, which shows how to take one core idea and sell it by many means simultaneously and/or continually.

So much for the "you" of writing. It takes somebody on the receiving end to buy your idea, then copy, and to convert it into cash. That is more likely, and easily, done if there is a reader as eager to buy the publication to see what you have to say as the editor is to buy your words so you can say it.

Timing almost always plays a key role in turning two or three of a kind into a winner.

While timing isn't what brings readers to books about Victorian romance, the West, intrigues of the Chou dynasty and similar date-pegged magazine pieces that have a timeless, universal appeal, what excites most readers and compels editors to buy is cutting-edge stuff, particularly in newspapers where the driving word is "new." Not the skyline of Paris but today's Parisian skyline. Not diseases but the newest DNA snippet that will lead to a cure in shingles or schizophrenia. Not just jokes or joking as a profession but how humor enriches corporate life or the Post Office.

Is your local primary school providing free lunches for volunteer seniors who will "grandpa" or "grandma" the students during the lunch recess? Is a federal forest preserve deasphalting the old parking lots and returning the center lands to wildflower preserves? Are the junior high schoolers setting up an Internet pen-pal link with a matching school in Nepal or Iceland or Angola? Those ideas sell. What they have in common is their "newness"—the one characteristic editors constantly seek for their pages. The time is almost always right for a good idea based on newness.

The second element to add to newness is appropriateness to the buyers of respective publications. The *Camel Drivers Gazette* would jump at the offer of articles about new breeds of camels to drive, new routes, new techniques, new tools. But even more tried pieces about "how to become a camel driver" or "how the old-timers drove their camels crazy" (or the reverse) would be far more welcome than query suggestions about hobo picnics or America's best mutual funds.

Another time consideration centers on holidays or specific events. Editors grow ecstatic at the prospect of finding holiday articles written to their peculiar readers about the themes of their publications, such as an article about barbershop quartets that visit homes to sing love songs on Valentine's Day, usually booked by husbands to warble three-song personal telegrams to their wives (for $25 donations to the Heart Fund)—written for a state barbershop magazine.

Chapter three continues the theme of topic timeliness.

It's a perfect match when the editor is salivating to buy the very thing you are frothing to sell—and you have the savvy and skill to provide what you promise.

CHAPTER TWO

The Selling Process

Let's begin by describing the steps it takes to sell then write a magazine article. In subsequent chapters, we will focus on newspaper sales and how you get an editor to buy your nonfiction book. Understanding the magazine process will make selling in the other media far easier.

Selling your article to a magazine editor

An overview first. Think of selling to editors as a game. They have the need, the print space and the money. Your job is to play detective and figure out how you can meet their need, fill their space and graciously accept their money.

You may have the words, ideas, brainpower and skill to do that, but that's not enough. You also need a selling system because a thousand other folks (some of them reading these very words) can also write, have good ideas and are just as eager as you are to tap those editors' coffers.

We've already described editors and their goal of finding good copy. Their space varies, but a typical magazine might buy six to ten articles from freelancers per month. Some will get the nod over you because they have proven to the editor that what they write works, is accurate and requires little or no editing or rewriting. You are probably fighting for one of four article slots per month, sometimes fewer.

The editor may pay from $200 to $4,000 per article (most are in the $300–$850 bracket), usually on a rough sliding scale that increases one or several hundred dollars for each subsequent sale. You start by writing on speculation ("Send it. If it works, I'll buy it."). After a few sales, you usually get an assignment, subject to a kill fee (often 33 to 50 percent of the original amount) if it's not bought. You might haggle over expenses later, but you have no leverage at the outset.

So the first thing you must know is what those editors might buy from you. Then whether it's worth your effort for what they pay.

You also need a means of getting your potential article before the editor's eyes. Even better, to get an early indication from that editor as to whether the finished piece, if prepared as proposed, would be favorably received. In other words, an indication that you're on a buying track before you commit the bulk of your time and expense gathering the final copy.

Knowing what the editor might buy from you, whether you can gather enough information to write it, which editors you should approach and in which order, the amount of space they have open for freelancers and if their pay warrants serious consideration are all the results of a two-pronged feasibility study. The first prong asks whether it is feasible to sell that article once it is written. The second asks whether it is feasible to write that article in the first place.

Once you know that both are feasible, your goal is to get your topic before the editor's eyes before actually writing the first word of the article. You do this for almost all magazines, by writing the aforementioned query letter. This one-page letter to the editor sells an idea and shows, in the selling, that you are the person to write the final prose for her pages. More about queries later.

Feasibility study: Is it feasible to sell?

You should expect to get paid for your writing. You are creating valuable property. You should be paid for your skills, time and energy, if not for the value it has for those printing and reading it.

Alas, you will only be paid if an editor recognizes your idea's worth and has the space and inclination to use it. So that's where your first deductive skills must be directed.

Write down, in one sentence, what your article will be about. (If you can't reduce it to one clear sentence, your topic needs tighter refinement before going further.) For example, in chapter six we will read a query letter about dementia. For that example, our sentence might be "This article will be a state-of-the-art piece about dementia: definition, risk factors, current research findings, treatment and home care."

Then make a list of the kind of people who would buy a magazine to read an article about that topic. Use your imagination here. When you think of that topic, who is involved with it? Who does it affect? Who hates it? Who is its champion? What kinds of people, jobs, professions, laws, institutions, equipment or other factors come to mind? Does that jar loose another kind of reader who would find your words interesting, threatening, exciting, appalling or otherwise particularly worth reading?

Sometimes lists of magazines or magazine categories remind you of the kinds of readers there are. The table of contents in the current *Writer's Market* can be used that way. So can the periodicals list at a library. Even a quick thumbing through the *Readers' Guide to Periodical Literature* or computer equivalent reveals categories easily forgotten.

List each of those kinds of readers who might buy the magazine containing your article. Then shuffle your list, putting the most interested first and the least interested last. Keep similar kinds of buyers bunched together by category. A partial list of potential buyers for articles about dementia (other than the demented) might look like this:

adults, general populace
medical readers
science readers
seniors
health care readers

Finally, what kinds of magazines do those people read? Where would they go to find your article? List those magazines seeking freelance articles that cater to those kinds of buyers. *Writer's Market* is the best source of editors and magazines actively seeking freelance writing. Using your prioritized list of readers by probable interest, find the categories of magazines where those readers would turn to find your words. Then, next to each potential kind of reader, list those magazines

Some magazines not listed in *Writer's Market* will buy freelance material and pay a decent rate. You can find the names of additional publications that might be potential markets on the racks in the supermarket or newsstand, on the periodicals list or in *Ulrich's International Periodicals Directory*. Send them a note indicating that you have an article idea in mind that you think their readers might enjoy and inquire if they buy freelance material. If so, would they send you either a "writer's guideline sheet" or any particulars you should know before querying, such as article length and payment rate? Make sure your writing is exemplary (or why would they bother to reply?). Also include an SASE for a response.

that seem appropriate (using their descriptions as the initial determinants).

While you are researching, see where similar articles have been in print in the past three years. Head for the subject index in the library's *Readers' Guide to Periodical Literature* (or the computer equivalent) and list all articles identical or close to your topic so you can return to them later to study their contents in full detail. For now, though, just pluck the highlights from them you need to make your query letter work.

Analyze closely those that are very similar to what you want to sell. Editors don't want close rewrites or content look-alikes of other articles recently in print. See how your approach differs, then focus on that in your query. Though related to other information in print, sell a clearly new slant or focus.

What kind of information should you note by those publications that you think might buy your article? The people you should contact—articles editor, managing editor, etc.—with their names, titles and addresses; how they pay (acceptance or publication); how much they pay or the range ("we start at $400 and pay as high as $750"); the number of issues per year; the percent of freelance material the editor buys; the article length or range ("our articles range from 800 to 1,300 words"); and any mention of seasonal or special topic use ("we use cooking guides and recipes only in the Christmas issues, which are prepared in May" or "we visit Europe in the spring, Asia in the fall").

When does the editor pay?

The most important consideration is *when* the editor pays. If it's on acceptance, that means the editor will either pay when the article has been approved (accepted) or within thirty days of that time, when the firm generates checks. Whether or not the article appears in print (almost all do), you have been paid for your skills and labor.

On the other hand, if an editor pays on publication, it means you will not be paid until the piece has been in print, and often not too quickly thereafter. The manuscript can sit unused and unusable (by you for reprints) for months or years. Sometimes those publications fold and you're not informed. Or editors leave, policies change and your words continue to sit, awaiting approval. Your wallet is similarly ignored.

So it follows that you should only query publications that pay on acceptance. You can send reprints (second rights) submissions to publications that pay on publication, accepting the delay and a lower pay rate as a trade-off for being able to have the same article used again without modification or with few, modest changes. (More about reprints in chapter twelve.)

Therefore, draw a line across a sheet of paper and above the line, list all those potential buying editors who pay on acceptance. Below the line, for later use, note those who pay on publication.

Then note the amount each publication pays, the frequency of publication (number of issues per year), the percentage of freelance material it uses, the article length and anything else that affects the order and consideration. The purpose of compiling this information is to create a market list so you can put the best potential buyers in order (we'll prioritize them later). Part of our list, in chart form, might look like the example on the following page.

What if your topic could be sold to many different markets?

Often there are many categories of potential readership, thus many lists of possible articles, each coming at the topic from distinct angles. In those cases, if you approached the editors of the various categories with clearly different article slants or topics, you could send out queries

Publication	a/p?	$ pay	# of issues	free-lance %	article length	other
Parade	a	$2,500+	wkly	90	800–1,500	3-mth fact lead
USA Weekend	a	$2,000	wkly	70	50–2,000	sidebar OK
Health	a	$1,800	7/yr	25 mss/yr	1,200	get guidelines before querying
Your Health	p	$25–$200	6/yr	70	300–2,000	
McCall's	a	high	mthly	200–300 mss yr	1,500–2,000	to exec ed
Grit	p	$150–$500	mthly?	60	1,200–1,500	3rd person/family

simultaneously about clearly different articles.

Let's say that our topic could easily be subdivided into three distinct angles, each most salable to a different readership. In that case, we would develop three lists in chart form from which we could create three different queries about three different topics. For example, we may develop one list on the general theme of dementia. A second approach might be ways one can detect Alzheimer's disease, both years before and as the symptoms appear, plus a review of opinions as to the advisability of that early detection. The third, a much closer look at what's called the Nun Study, and the possibility that in early adult writing, we see indications that the root of Alzheimer's may already exist. In each case, we would create a chart like that above, or reassign the general list of potential publications to the most likely selling category.

The only advice here is that on the rare chance that the same magazine might fall on more than one list, don't send two competing queries to the same editor. Give the poor soul time to accept or reject the most appropriate idea before returning again.

How much does the editor pay?

It matters. If it's $10 for 10,000 words, that's the fast path to penury. Here, you are more interested in comparative rates to help you determine which editors you wish to court in which order.

Alas, sometimes you simply don't know. *Writer's Market* might not list a payment amount or say "to be arranged" and you can't guess from other payments listed for that magazine. (You could call the magazine and ask.)

Or it may give only a range, say, $400–$800. If you're new to that publication, figure it will be $400, unless you are writing the key feature or you bring something special to the page that might boost the rate (like celebrity, first-hand heroic experience or you are the editor's mother).

How often does the magazine publish?

A magazine that uses 100 percent freelance but publishes every decade loses to one that uses 10 percent freelance and publishes twice a year!

Most magazines are monthlies. Again, the more often the magazine sees light, the better your chances of selling to it.

What percentage of material used is bought from freelancers?

Some magazines are 100 percent freelance written, excluding the stock copy and ads. Most fall in the 65 to 85 percent category. Many smaller publications have an editor who selects and modestly edits the articles from the public, plus one or several assistant editors who write everything else.

But you must check on this before making any assumptions because there are magazines that buy rarely, don't want to be bothered by freelancers and consider anything submitted as fodder to be used only in dire emergency.

Again, *Writer's Market* is a good guide here—or the "guidelines for writers" sent by the publication.

The higher the percentage, the better your chance.

What's the best, or suggested, article length?

Of all the classifications, this is the least important, assuming that the editor doesn't confuse an article with a book.

That's mentioned only for the sake of comparison. A $50 article containing 8,000 words will leave a different taste in your mouth and imprint on your wallet than a $2,500 article of 2,500 words.

But there may be situations where the first is a dream come true and the second, nice but just another job.

Other selling considerations

Many other things can affect the order of consideration.

Some are personal: You can't ethically or morally write about a certain topic or have your words appear on certain pages; you disagree with a magazine's policy, its advertisers, they way it treats a particular gender or sex; or you would be embarrassed to have your byline between its covers.

Some are professional: You work for the competing firm, or the personal reasons above spread into the professional field and affect the publication as well.

Some are economic, beyond the pay rate and method: You'll be traveling in a certain area and it would make dollar sense to write the piece for a lower-paying magazine that is more interested in that locale, or you'd simply rather write for a nonpaying philanthropic publication, income loss notwithstanding.

It's your life, your time, your energy, your skills, your choice.

Prioritizing your market list

What do we do with this newly created font of information, as it pertains to our article about dementia? Let's put all six publications in the best selling order, using, again, as our criteria, when the editor pays, how much, the frequency of publication, the percent of freelance material used, article length, plus any other considerations. The result is a prioritized market list, like the example on the next page, that will guide our querying and reprint marketing selling.

For now, set aside the last two since they pay on publication. It's not worth our time to query them for original work. We'll consider them for reprints later, after the original article appears in print.

We will query the first four in the order listed, beginning with the editor of the top selection. If that query is rejected, we'll study the second market, rewrite the query to match that editor's needs and send it to the editor of number two. And so on, until an editor gives us a positive response or we run out of publications and editors that pay on acceptance to whom we wish to submit our work.

Publication	a/p?	$ pay	# of issues	free-lance %	article length	other
McCall's	a	high	mthly	200–300 mss/year	1,500–2,000	to exec ed
Parade	a	$2,500+	wkly	90	800–1,500	3-mth fact lead
USA Weekend	a	$2,000	wkly	70	50–2,000	sidebar OK
Health	a	$1,800	7/yr	25 mss/yr	1,200	get guidelines before querying
Grit	p	$150–$500	mthly?	60	1,200–1,500	3rd person/family
Your Health	p	$25–200	6/yr	70	300–2,000	

Of course, should the query be accepted by any of the first four, we could find a different angle or slant to the topic that would result in a clearly different article and we could send that query to the remaining pay-on-acceptance publications, in order. (Madness proliferates: We could even send out five clearly different query letters simultaneously to all five of the markets as long as the resulting articles are so distinct that none of the editors would feel that we just lightly reworked his bought masterpiece and sold it to the competition.)

You have the starting information; now you need the selling tools

To sell, you needed to know which editors might buy from you, whether they had space for your article and whether the effort was worth the pay. You also needed a means of getting your potential article before the editor's eyes so you would know if you were on a buying track before you committed the bulk of your time and expense to gathering and writing the final copy.

Your prioritized market list answers the first three concerns. Your query letter will put the idea before the editor, and the editor's response will let you know if further pursuit will likely lead to a published and paid conclusion.

Since this book dedicates a full chapter to query letters—they are the single most important tool used by freelance writers—this is as far as we'll go for now to see if it's feasible to sell your idea to a magazine editor.

But an equally important question remains: Even if you can sell it, is it feasible to write the article that you propose to sell? Keep your detective hat firmly tied. There's more digging to do.

Feasibility study: Is it feasible to write?

You don't want to fully research and write a whole article, then reduce that to a one-page query to see if the editor is even interested enough to ask you to fully research and write a whole article!

It only makes sense to conduct a short investigation of the topic, gathering highlights or key information to help the editor decide if she needs more to give you a go-ahead for the full submission. You submit that information in your best writing style so the editor can evaluate the topic and see if your writing is of sufficient quality to result in a salable article.

In other words, form-fit a topic to the editor's needs, pluck out its most salient characteristics, present the idea and the main points in your best prose in a one-page query letter and ask if you should devote the remaining time and skill to completing the concept in finished article form.

So to successfully conduct this segment of the two-pronged feasibility study, you would need to conclude that the topic would result in an article the editor would buy, then present the key information supporting that conclusion to the editor for an initial, affirmative response.

Topic confirmation

You have four critical tasks to perform at this stage.

The first is to find a topic you believe the purveyors of your target publication would eagerly read, and thus would be bought by the editor to use on his pages. It's immaterial whether you pick a topic first, then find magazines with readers who would eagerly read it, or you find the magazine first, then deduce from its readership what you think they would eagerly read. We speak about topic selection in depth in chapter three.

The second task is to see if that magazine has recently used articles about this or a closely related topic. If so, that could yield two conclusions: (1) the readers' interest was probably satisfied and the editor won't soon return to that topic, directly or by extension, or (2) the topic is every bit as compelling now as it was after the article appeared and the editor may well want more—a continuation from where the article ended, an update, a broader "state-of-the-art" piece, a different slant or some other copy coming from the topic in question. An example might be an article about levee construction during the dry season to prevent further erosion during the spring thaw, followed by a detailed article seven months later after a devastating flood that asks, and answers, "Did the levees hold?"

If (2) is your conclusion, then this second step requires you to identify the approach you will use to again sell that editor on a topic previously or recently bought. If it is (1), you must either find another publication that hasn't covered the topic but you believe would like to or you must find a different topic.

The third task is to research the topic.

I'm not suggesting weeks or months of tome dust, Internet slavery or nationwide pavement pounding, rather a few hours of defining, zeroing in, verifying and selecting. After all, you only need to produce about three or four paragraphs—the core of a query letter—of captivating copy to get the yea or nay. (Later, when you get the nod, you will complete the research, as long as it takes, and convert that into a meticulously written full manuscript.)

But at this point, you must be able to answer a key question: "If I send this query to the editor and get a yes, can I write the article?" If so, you must also gather enough good, pertinent information to fill those few query paragraphs.

That means that as you read the articles or other sources in print about your topic and note the facts, anecdotes and people quoted, you also set aside those key gems you will use in your query. In addition, you note where you will find more information, which you may share with the editor in that query.

Remember that your query letter will be written like the article to follow, in style and tone. So if the article will be light and quick, you will need to inject wit and fast facts. If it will be full of quotes tied to bullets, your research must unearth quotes and bullets. Those three or four paragraphs must both show and tell, so your hours of probing must be directed to produce model snippets of what the article will display and develop in full.

The last task is to get into both the soul of that target magazine and the mind of its buying editor, convert your chosen facts and preferred angle or slant into copy akin to that sought by the publication's readers and write a query letter that successfully sells your topic.

That explains what you must do to know enough to write the selling query letter. You need a positive reply to both feasibility questions: Is it feasible to sell? And is it feasible to write? If it is, you query the editor of the top magazine on your prioritized market list, and should that bring a rejection, you query the editor of the second and so on.

How can you remember all that? And how do you know what to do in what order? A checklist is provided, beginning on the next page, that you can use to become familiar with the process. It hits the critical elements more or less in the order they actually occur. When you get a positive reply, you will complete steps 12–15.

Study the other articles your editor just bought

First, let's discuss in fuller detail what you want to know before you write the article or even the query letter that would make writing that article a possibility. If you want to sell to an editor, study closely what that editor recently bought, wrap your idea and prose in similar garb, keep it about the same length (unless instructed otherwise), and you are flirting with a paycheck.

You can't simply rewrite copy from the last issue and plop your name in the byline. So what are you looking for?

A close study of earlier articles will tell all. Find the last three issues of the magazine in which you want to appear; select at least one article from each that is as close to the topic, style, format, even length of the piece that you want to write.

You do this to find that formula from which the editor does not stray (at the risk of losing readers, irking the publisher and starting the slippery slide to ex-editorship) that is defined by topic, words and style. Create a hypothetical mental box within which that editor must stay—and into which your copy must fit.

How to Prepare and Market Articles That Sell

1. In one sentence, what is the subject of the article you want to write and sell?

2. Who would benefit from reading your article? Who would be most interested? What kinds of readers would select your specific subject from a variety of choices? Rank all those potential readers in order, placing those who would derive the most benefits first.

3. Which publications do these readers buy and read? Prepare a market list of those publications that are the most likely to buy your manuscript.

4. In addition to the publications checked in (3), it is necessary to review the broader publishing field for articles similar or identical to yours. Therefore, you must check both the *Readers' Guide to Periodical Literature*, or the computer equivalent, and specific subject indexes for at least the previous three years. Then list the articles that are closest to your subject, with the most similar first, and record each article's subject, author, title, publication, page reference, length and date of publication. Cross-check newspaper indexes for the past three years and provide the same information.

5. If the publications listed in (3) and (4) have printed articles within the past three years that are similar to the one you propose, how precisely does your differ? You must highlight that difference in your query letter.

6. After each publication, note the name of the person you should contact (editor, managing editor, etc.), with title and address. Then provide the following information about each publication:
   a. Does it pay on acceptance or publication?
   b. How much does it pay for articles as long as yours?
   c. How often is it published?
   d. What percentage of it is written by freelancers?
   e. What is its preferred manuscript length?
   f. Is any other information provided that will affect its placement on your list?

7. Now rank your market list in priority order, based on when the buyers pay (on acceptance or on publication), how much, the frequency of publication and the percentage of freelance material used per issue.

8. Read the latest issue of your target publication, front to back. Better yet, the last three issues. Select at least one article from each issue as close to, in form if not topic, the piece you wish to write. Outline each article. Write out the lead and conclusion of each, by hand. Follow the twelve steps in "How to Study a Printed Magazine Article" on page 31. Attempt to identify the publication's readers by age, sex, occupation, income range, education, residence and other pertinent factors.

9. To verify the availability of resource information
   a. read as many of the articles in (5) as necessary or possible, then list the sources of information found in each,
   b. consult the card catalog and list the books you will refer to for factual information: title, author, call number, date of publication and library, and
   c. list the people you should consult for additional information and quotes, working with the reference librarian for information you do not already have: their names, positions, current affiliations (if related to the topic), academic titles and degrees (if relevant) and reasons for their being consulted.

10. From the information you've gathered on the specific target publication and the research you've done on your topic, select the material needed to write a professional query letter. Verify its accuracy.

11. Write a selling query letter to an editor of your target publication. If you do not receive a positive reply, write a query letter to the editor of the next publication on your list and so on, one editor at a time, until an editor does respond positively. Repeat as much of (9) as necessary for each new publication queried.

12. When you receive that positive response to your query, plan your article to determine what is still needed to finish it.

13. Complete the needed research.
14. Write the manuscript in final draft form. Include, on separate paper, at least five additional, different leads. Then pick the best and adjust your article to make it work.
15. Edit the draft, print a final manuscript (keeping a copy in your file) and mail the manuscript (or send it on computer disk, if requested by the editor), with illustrations (if needed and available), to the editor who gave you the go-ahead.

The topics covered. Why does the magazine exist? What is its purpose? Who are its readers? The box contains information they want or need to know. It excludes anything irrelevant to their lives or interests.

A magazine for ultramarathoners discusses training, diet, racing flats, running attire, workout schedules, health concerns for long-distance runners, races, carbohydrate packing, dehydration and hundreds of other ultramarathoning concerns. It does not include articles about newts, nuclear fission, *The Simpsons*, Iraq or men as Martians.

When in doubt, read the table of contents for the past three issues, or the index for the last year or two.

If you wish to write about a topic already covered, ask yourself why the editor would want to use it again. Do you have important new information? A timely, needed follow-up? A critical update? A different slant that ultramarathoners would greatly benefit from knowing?

Conversely, what hasn't been written about that ultramarathoners need to know? If you can show the editor why your new information is important, timely and needed, here is your greatest chance of breaking onto those pages, particularly if, at the same time, you show that there is enough information for a solid article and you show the verbal dexterity to be able to write it.

The farther the topic is from the readers' and editor's core interest, the harder one must work to show why it should be on the target pages—effort usually spent in vain.

The words used and style employed. Since the editor's writing-buying box contains only those words the editor deems appropriate to her readership, there are several things to consider when determining which words to use for respective publications.

The first is the most obvious: In what language is the publication written?

If not English, do you write the other language at the level used by the editor? If so, submit it as is. If not, will the editor be able to read your query and copy in English? And will that editor have it well and faithfully translated for you? Does that come out of your payment?

Since this book is in English, presumably most of its readers will be writing for publications using English. But again, which version of English? U.S. standard or derivations of the mother tongue, with its *labours* and *petrol*? If the latter, it's best to write in U.S. standard and let the editors in England, Australia, South Africa or elsewhere make the modest adaptations that will make their readers feel more at home with the final text.

Even U.S. standard isn't so standard. There's a considerable gap in word selection, pace and purpose between William Buckley's measured prose and the swashbuckling, foul-mouthed banter of the more raucous detective novels and pithy magazines. Regionalisms, dialects and levels of abstraction play a role too.

So questions must be asked about who reads the pages on which you want to appear, why they read them, how much book learning and/or hands-on experience they bring to the task and what they expect to see on those pages.

What you can include in your article can be deduced by seeing what others included in theirs. Others' articles are available to study in past issues. If you want to see what the editor buys, see what she bought the past few months. If you want to sell to that editor, write in a similar style and use similar words.

Some words are outside the box and will disqualify you immediately. Writing for children? Graphically explicit sexual descriptions are well outside the box. For sewing magazines? Gang slang won't work. But hippie, experimental, earthy works? The box may be big enough to include almost anything writable.

More than taboo words, phrases and concepts, studying the context will tell you what you should consider including. If the article three issues back had four people interviewed, the next had four people interviewed and the article from the last issue also had four people interviewed, you might seriously consider including four interviews in your article.

Why? Because the editor obviously feels comfortable with that balance. If you want to include three or five? That might still work, but none or twelve misses by a mile.

Look closer yet. Were those four quotes from top authorities or experts in the field? Or were they average readers giving their opinions or homespun knowledge? Was there a mixture? Were the quotes long and detailed, or were they short, each making one sharp point? These are more clues about what the editor seeks that can help you better define where you must look for your quotes and how extensive the hunt must be.

How is the article structured? Is it one long point developed brick by brick, chronologically, geographically or by some other means? Is the theme divided into three main points, each a subheading, with those further subdivided?

How are the facts in the article presented? As bullets? As lists? As sidebars to highlight key aspects or isolate and magnify specific quotes? Are the details pinpoint specific: exact dates, routes, times, instructions? Or are they very general, allowing the reader to add the specifics? A mix of the two?

How many sentences are there in the paragraphs? How many paragraphs to a section? How many words in total?

There's no reason for any writer to operate in a vacuum or void. The editors tell what they buy through what they have bought. All the potential writer of future articles must do is read the bought articles carefully, determine what style and content the editors include in their boxes and stay within those confines when he composes his piece.

Does this suck the creativity from new writers? Hardly. It simply says to be as creative as the topic and readership allow within the confines of the editor's buy box!

How do you know what that editor expects in the final manuscript— and the query?

Is there anything else that will help you zero in even more tightly on what that editor is seeking? Or that will help you write a query more in the style of the later article, short of writing the article first? You

How to Study a Printed Magazine Article

1. Read closely each article in recent issues of the magazine to which you are trying to sell. Most contain an answer to a basic working question. Identify that question. How does the article answer it? Which of the "5 *w*'s and *h* of journalism" does it use: who, what, why, where, when and how?

2. Now read the entry for that publication in *Writer's Market* for the year of (or preceding) the article's appearance. Working backward from the question answered and the indications in *Writer's Market* of what that magazine was seeking, try to put yourself in the writer's shoes. How did the writer slant the subject to appeal to the magazine's readers? Why did the editor buy it? Study its structure, length, illustrations and artwork.

3. To see how the writer carries the main theme through the article, underline each word that relates directly to that theme, then outline the entire piece. Study the writer's use of facts, quotes and anecdotes. What is the ratio between them? How is humor used? Is it spread and balanced to the same degree throughout? Do other articles in this issue use facts, quotes, anecdotes and humor in roughly the same way and in the same proportion?

4. List every source used, including direct references and quotations. Where would the writer find the facts, opinions and quotes that are not clearly identified by source in the article? If you are uncertain, indicate where you would find the material— or where you would go to find out.

5. Focus on the quotations. Why is each used? How does it carry the theme forward? Note how the source of the quotation is introduced, and how much the reader must know about the source to place the person and what is said in perspective.

6. Is the article written in first person (*I*), second (*you*) or third (*he*, *she*, *it* or "Mr. Smith")? How does that strengthen the article? Does the point of view change? Why or why not? Are most other articles in the same issue written in the same person?

7. Concentrate on the lead. How long is it, in words or sentences? Does it grab your interest? Does it make you want to read more? Why? How does it compare with other leads in that issue?

8. Most articles begin with a short lead followed by a longer second paragraph that ties the lead to the body of the article. Called the *transitional paragraph*, it tells where you are going and how you will get there. It bridges the attention-grabbing elements of the lead to the expository elements of the body by setting direction, tone and pace. Find the transitional paragraph and study it.

9. Now underline the first sentence in each paragraph. They should form a chain that will pull you through the piece. Note how the writer draws the paragraphs together with transitional words and phrases. Circle the words that perform this linking function. Often the same words or ideas will be repeated in the last sentence of one paragraph and the first sentence of the next.

10. Earlier you outlined the article. Now look at the transitional words and the underlined first sentences and see how the structure ties the theme together. Is the article structured chronologically, developmentally, by alternating examples, point by point? How did the writer build the organizational structure to answer the article's question?

11. How does the article end? Does it tie back to the lead? Does it repeat an opening phrase or idea? The conclusion should reinforce and strengthen the direction that article has taken. Does it? How?

12. Finally, look at the title. It may have been changed or rewritten by the editor. Nonetheless, does it correctly describe the article that follows? Does it tease, quote, pique one's curiosity, state facts? What technique does it use to make the reader want to read the article?

bet. It's an analytical reading tool summarized in the twelve steps that follow. Though it's called "How to Study a Printed Magazine Article," it can as easily and profitably be used to study newspaper articles or books. You *must* use it if you get a go-ahead, before you write the final copy. But smart freelancers apply it earlier, before they submit those make-or-break query letters.

Ideas

Now that we have an action plan for a magazine article, we need something to act around: an idea at the heart of our article.

Editors buy ideas, information, something readable that meets their publishing needs. If the writing isn't usable as is, they can edit it or direct it to be rewritten, to make it work. But if the *idea* doesn't meet their needs, the quality of the writing is irrelevant: It simply won't be bought for their pages, however dazzling or drab.

In other words, to get an editor to buy your prose, it must say something worth buying and sharing with the readers. The sales success of an article you want to write, the kind of publication you want to sell it to (magazine, newspaper or book) and its purchasability by the specific publication depend overwhelmingly upon one thing: what it is about. You must start with an idea that those particular readers, and thus editors, want to know (more) about.

In summary, sought ideas equal selling articles.

So let's develop a system for finding sought ideas.

One way is to head for the library. You can simply look at the tables of contents in magazines or you can see what topics were written about, and where, by consulting the *Readers' Guide to Periodical Literature* or its computerized counterpart. For the more specialized or academic magazines and journals, see other indexes for almost every academic field: business, foreign languages, psychology, nursing, etc. Your reference librarian will point the way.

Writer's Digest is also available at most libraries and runs an occasional list of new article ideas. But I do wonder about the despair editors must feel when pounds of query letters arrive on their desks containing those concepts! If you think up your own, you are your only competition!

Perhaps the most provocative source is *Writer's Market*, which makes clear suggestions for almost every magazine cited.

Finally, for fun browsing, go to the index of *The New York Times* or *Los Angeles Times* (or any other major metro newspaper) and just see the kinds of things others have written about for those newspapers. Often you can combine some of those topics to create an idea uniquely yours, which you can then share, lucratively, with an editor and his readers.

There are at least ten more ways to find topics for articles that sell that will help you get to where the professionals are.

Ideas abound. Let's figure out how to find them.

Everyday things

Let me pose a heretical thought: Almost any idea or topic will sell—if you are willing to hunt hard enough for an editor eager to use it and willing enough to accept whatever she will pay, if anything.

Not what you had in mind? You're right. You don't want to sell just any idea for little or no income. You want to find ideas for articles eagerly sought that will earn you enough to make your effort worthwhile.

The good news is those ideas are the easiest to find. They're right in front of you: They're the common, everyday things you see, think of, talk about, feel and fear.

Beginners think they need something unique or bizarre or special to write about to get into print. In fact, it's just the reverse, if they are to sell an idea often and well. What editors want are the things that people—their readers—think and talk about all the time.

The best article ideas are related to comfort, survival, fear, anxiety, hope, love, joy, security, curiosity, even death. And what do all of these have in common? They're concerns of readers. Consciously or unconsciously, they are the threads of our everyday existence; they are what any reader most wants to know about.

Don't write an article that complains solely and at length about your snoring spouse. Write a broad article about snoring spouses, with a half-dozen examples, causes and cures, and enough emotion that the reader will thank God his spouse doesn't—or nod tiredly at every word, in instant recognition.

Don't write about divorce in Denmark; write about "How to Mend Your Marital Fence." Don't write about Freud and dreams; show how your readers' dreams can be paths to a better tomorrow.

Use your own frequency of thought as a gauge. If you think of the same thing every week, write about it—you've probably got a money-maker. And if you think of that topic every day, you've got a gold mine. (Of course, if you think of it five times a day, you have an obsession!)

At the cost of redundancy (worse yet, repetitious redundancy): Readers want to read about themselves. Most people, by their perceptions, lead plain, straightforward lives. So write about the components of such lives: jobs, family, school, playtime, dreams, mental and physical concerns, physical and emotional drives.

You may be thinking to yourself, *That's been done to death; that's all I read about!* But that's precisely why you do read about it. It's what the editors must share to meet their readers' demands.

The trick is to find a new angle, an update, a different application. Let's focus on a topic that seems to be permanent copy in the publications we see most often on the newsstands: divorce. There are always new items to add to the reader's basic stock of information here: new laws, new property allocations, new ways of handling custody, new studies showing different effects upon each person or both parties, new attitudes, new views by church and state, new reasons for divorcing, new tax ramifications, new legal means of filing and separating. On and on. All you have to do is add the angle or research or revelation or study results to the old base and you have a different, "new" article about divorce. That holds true for virtually any subject that is part of a reader's life.

The last thought in that vein: There are writers who spend their lifetimes writing about one subject. They do just what I said. First they read everything written; then they find ways to capture new information quickly, much before it sees print. Finally, as their names become identified with specific topics, participants in those fields turn to those same writers when there is something for print. The key word is always *new*.

What's even better, the common ideas, those that are most sought by the highest paying publications, are also the ones that will earn you the most.

Here's an example, in reverse. In Ecuador I found pockets of animated locals engaged in an exciting but largely unknown sport called *pelota de guante*, literally "glove ball," which was brought to that part of the world by the Spaniards in the 1500s. It is a precursor of volleyball and is played near Quito on 60-foot grass courts with a 3-pound rubber ball and huge, 20-pound leather gloves with giant nail heads in them. I queried virtually every known magazine interested in sports or travel about *pelota de guante*, adding that I also had excellent color slides. Still, using successful selling techniques that have now worked 1,600+ times, the subject appeared in print but twice—earning a total of $130. It's a perfect example of the fact that the odd, off-center pieces are one-shot sales, or at most two- or three-, and seldom make their authors much money.

Common topics—children, second careers, pets, cures and loneliness—are the things of which many sales and big money come. Really.

So your job is less one of finding ideas (look around you!) than of finding new and different ways to rework everyday themes.

Matching the target publication's approach

There are two basic approaches to idea finding: (1) the first would have you out hunting for the ideas, and later searching for publications that might use them, while (2) the second would have you study specific publications to see the kinds of ideas used to meet their readers' needs, then match article concepts to those publications' styles, lengths and formats. The more you write, the more you will find yourself doing some of both, with the emphasis shifting to the latter as you develop a cadre of magazines for which you write most often.

Let me zero in on three publications to illustrate both key points: that their contents are full of everyday things and it is far easier to study a magazine first, guess what its readers want to read and then match an article idea to the way that magazine's articles are written.

The three are the November 1996 issues of *Harper's Bazaar, Travel Holiday* and *Seventeen*, a broad selection of general magazines directed at clearly different readerships: women, travelers and teenagers (overwhelmingly female—most teenage boys aren't avid readers anyway, particularly of *Seventeen*!)

What would you expect women readers of *Harper's Bazaar* to want on that magazine's pages? Style, beauty, health—subjects about or affecting women. Those are what I call everyday, expected things. And what does this issue talk about?

The 39 articles or sections are divided into four categories: Fashion (with 15 articles), Beauty and Health (8), Features (9) and Departments (7). Bad news for aspiring freelance contributors. Only six carry bylines (usually indicating outside contributions), two from book reviewers. The rest appear to be staff written or inside assignments. Not a hotbed of outside sales.

Fashion is composed 100 percent of fashion-related pieces, Beauty and Health is likewise 100 percent beauty and health and there's nothing unexpected in the Departments section (Mastheads, Editor's Note, Contributors, Letters, People, Horoscopes and Buyline). Where would we find the radical, unexpected, new-insight piece? Features. Setting aside Art, Movies, Books and Design, we find a first-person article about Marion Winik and her "somewhat-soiled past"; Disney's daring, multidimensional approach to a Broadway adaptation of *The Lion King*; three career women who refuse to let men gerrymander the gender lines; the *new* Kristin Scott Thomas; and three famous (male!) architects who may forever change the L.A. landscape.

Travel Holiday is about—yep, you guessed it—travel and where to go on holiday! Twenty-one items in the November 1996 edition were lumped into two categories: Features (6 articles) and Departments (15).

The geographic range of the contents was wide enough, but the staff or contributing editors wrote eleven of the items, leaving the outsiders to handle bullfighting in Provence, the transfigured Myrtle Beach, voodoo in the Caribbean, the posh Canyon Ranch in Arizona, Belgium, three small hotels in the Twin Cities, Tahiti, a look at the migrating monarch butterflies, another regal piece about QE2, and Old San Juan. Not bad and a good spread, but what makes each article work is its strict adherence to the publication theme and title: travel and holiday, with plenty of affluence thrown in.

Seventeen is precisely what you'd expect: lots of girl talk. What would a seventeen-year-old young woman read in November? A wide assortment of things—37—divided into predictable categories: Fashion and Beauty (11 articles), Bodyline (1), The Spin (2), Voice (1), Drive (1), Guys (3), Scene (6), Features (4), Eat (2) and Columns (6). But only fifteen bylines, and of those seven were written by staffers and two more by contributing editors. Less than one-sixth of the total (six articles) are freelanced.

Sample titles? "A Time to Chill: Kick Back and Relax in All-American Classic Clothes," "Motor Mouth: Does He Love You for Your Car?" and "The Scoop on Older Guys. I Was a Freshman. He Was a Senior. Was Our Relationship Doomed From the Start?"

Where do you look for something to write about for *Seventeen*? Inside the head, heart, glands and muscles of a seventeen-year-old young woman. Take inventory of her fears, hopes, embarrassments, joys, needs, wants and frustrations and see what hasn't been written about recently. Better yet, what *has* that you can do better, or to which you can add new information or provide new insight. Focus on the reader and study the pages, and what needs to be said is what you write about.

For those pages, forget "Teenage Puberty in Paraguay." Don't talk about Babe Ruth, the man or the candy bar. Forget exquisite, goofy, remote, unrelated items. Talk skin, eyes, college, dating, "How to Talk to a Boy."

Seeing article ideas from the perspective of the magazine's needs makes sense—and cents.

The five-angle approach

Let me add five more points of view to consider for each of your ideas. Note a subject you'd like to write an article about, then ask yourself how that idea would differ for infants, children, teenagers, honeymooners and retirees—in addition, of course, to your average reader in the age range of 20–50.

This five-angle approach is suggested by Louise Purwin Zobel in her excellent *The Travel Writer's Handbook*, so let's use a travel topic as an example to show how it might be applied to your idea seeking.

Say you want to visit Iceland. Is it wise to take infants with you? Is there proper food for them? Medical care should they take ill? Baby-sitting if you want to spend an evening, or days, touring alone? Similar questions are asked by every mother eager to visit any part of the world. So editors are interested too.

Much the same applies for youngsters. Beyond food and health concerns, and baby-sitting too, would they find other children to play with? Are there activities geared specifically to kids that they could enjoy? Must they attend school if it is in session? Are they safe on the streets alone? Plus at least a hundred more questions that traveling parents will have. When zeroing in on toddlers and kids, you are writing to the parents, of course.

Teens are a different market. More and more, they are traveling alone or in small groups, and the later teens, usually in college, thrive on seeing new places and people. So, what is there for them to do in Iceland? How well can they thrive with English as their only language? Are there restrictions because of their age? Must they be chaperoned? What are the local customs regarding alcohol, drugs and other temptations? In short, write to the teens about what's up for them in Iceland.

Honeymooners might not have Iceland at the top of their list, but what is there for them to enjoy on those special days of their lives? Ideal stuff for honeymooning and marriage magazines. And retirees? Great travelers, but sticklers on detail (cost, season, transportation) and alternative ways to see the sights without having to scale the peaks, swim the bays or leap across the geysers.

The point of all five: Put the target group—from tots to elders—in the center and build articles around them. Add travel and you have an easy selling combination.

A different setting or gender

While we are talking of travel, almost any "regular" story can gain a second life by changing its setting or by putting it in a different culture. Christmas in London. Surfing in South Africa, stamp collecting in Chad, watching a baseball game in Japan, driving across the United States—of Brazil. There's hardly a magazine that won't accept a story with a legitimate foreign angle. If you don't believe me, look for these creatures in the tables of contents of most major consumer magazines, then moan that somebody else did it first, had fun on the trip, got it paid for in writing earnings and also deducted the costs from her taxes!

Another easy mental switch is to take a fresh look at what were "male" or "female" articles, then generalize them or write them to include the opposite sex. The pieces about car maintenance for the housewife or baking for both breadwinners.

The newspaper

The best on-hand source for article ideas is surely the newspaper. It may seem paradoxical that you would take items from one medium and sell them to another or back to the newspapers themselves, but that is precisely what is done by professionals and novices in the know.

First, there are no "rights" problems. News is public domain, and you will be using the facts in a different order anyway. You won't simply send a clipping of a newspaper piece to an editor; rather you'll extract the most interesting elements, add more facts and create a new piece from a different angle.

News in the newspaper is an hour or a day old. Magazine articles seldom reach the stands in less than two months. Their copy is news converted into feature stories, with the particular news peg generally placed in a broader context, reslanted to stress that magazine's particular orientation and often combined with other facts, quotes and anecdotes to give the subject new life and enduring interest.

If you want to see this in action, check magazines and newspapers since the collapse of communism in the former U.S.S.R. That phenomenon first appeared on television, then in the newspapers, then the news weeklies (like *Time* and *Newsweek*) and finally the "regular" magazines with longer lead times. The difference was subtle: The television talked about the immediate impact on life in Russia or Georgia; the weeklies used the same facts as openers for pieces of greater depth; and the monthly magazines, seeing light many months after the "news" value had faded, offered an even broader perspective, deeper analysis, plus more and better photographs.

The best stories, though, are seldom as important or obvious as the collapse of communism. They are frequently the one- or two-paragraph items on page two or even page ten that suggest something bigger is afoot deserving closer attention.

Here's another example. In southern California, where a lack of rain and the scorching Santana winds create fire hazards, wood shake roofs are a menace. This is fairly well known locally. But if you see a couple of short pieces indicating that homes of about the same vintage, say, twenty years old, each caught fire in separate locations, starting on the same kinds of roofs, you might ask yourself if these roofs haven't reached a particularly dangerous level after x number of years of drying out. If you research further and discover that this was the most common style of roofing two decades back, you might have the kind of article that would catch many an editor's eye—and reader's wallet. The obvious articles, through possible titles:

"Time to Replace That Flammable Roof?"
"Fire-Hazard Roofs Reaching Their Danger Peak?"
"Shake Roofs Putting Neighborhoods in Peril?"
"Time to Require Fire Retardant on Shake Roofs?"

Who knows, with enough press exposure you might help prevent a fire or much of its disastrous aftermath, like the inferno near Disneyland that left two thousand people homeless from just that combination of physical causes.

Expanding on news shorts is a time-honored art of professional article writers. Once I kept seeing the same topic over and over, each time in a filler one or two paragraphs long; each spoke of animals finding their way home over long distances. I wondered to myself, *just how do animals do that?*, and while researching, I uncovered so much interesting information that I wrote it up and sold it over thirty times.

Dates or years

Dates or years are obvious pegs for future articles, though the date should be from six months to a year away to give yourself time for querying, for the research after you get a go-ahead and for sufficient lead time for the publication.

Let's use a date far enough past to show how you might have written about it. Say, 1985. In early 1984, you should have begun querying about articles for the next year, using the date as the reason for their being printed at that time.

There are various approaches to using a date or year to find both stories and markets. In 1985 you may have wished to sell articles with "100th anniversary" tie-ins, so you would begin by researching the year 1895. Lo and behold, that was the maiden year for *Good Housekeeping*, which might in fact be a super target for a general, fun but fact-filled piece about the year during which the first issue emerged.

Medical or health magazines might be interested in recognizing the hundredth anniversary of America's first successful appendectomy, or the world's first administration of antirabies vaccine. Johnson and Johnson also opened in 1895.

Gun fans will be interested in the centenary of the Browning single-shot rifle; any one of five colleges may want a general piece on 1885 for their alumni or general publications, because in that year Stanford, Georgia Tech, Bryn Mawr, McAlester and the University of Arizona began.

How has music changed since the first presentation of *The Mikado* or even *The Gypsy Baron*? England first adopted an identification system that year based on fingerprints, and America made the big time with the appearance of both Morton's salt and evaporated milk. And so on. Historical items of interest to be used alone, magnified by research or joined in a "Did you know?" piece in which the key items lead.

Incidentally, for the sources to such ideas, simply go to the library and ask for the "date" books. James Trager's *The People's Chronology* is excellent, but there are also *The Almanac of Dates*, *The Timetables of History* and many more.

Or you may wish to use 1985 as a pivotal year, with the *85* the unifying factor, and put together a historical collage of unique, interesting, sometimes comical, occasionally tragic events that took place in the centuries ending in *85*, say, 1085, 1485, 1785, 1885.

Let me share a final thought on this source of ideas. It is based on history, and history is death to magazine sales unless you can offset the readers' aversion to names and dates with other factors, such as humor, irony, new ways of seeing old facts and animated writing. Historical material must be full-fleshed, bigger than life almost, and the query in which you attempt to sell this idea must be extremely sharp and as lively as the article to follow. So dates and years are a mine of good material waiting to be unearthed, then revitalized.

Holidays

Related to dates are holidays, which are a true bane to editors weary of churning the same old ideas. Forget articles venerating Arbor Day or Groundhog Day, but if you can find new angles or slants to the evergreens—Christmas, New Year, Easter, Thanksgiving, Halloween, Valentine's and the Fourth of July—you'll probably have a sale. There's one catch, though: Most publications want holiday material at least six months in advance, and often Christmas material a year before. *Writer's Market* will clue you in.

There are two ways to go. First, review the earlier holiday issues and see what's already been done. If it's more than three to five years old, try a similar approach again, updated.

The second is to approach the holiday from one of these slants:

1. *Anecdotal approach*—Tie in well-known names, of the present or past, with the event: Teddy Roosevelt's Christmas, Don Rickles's Halloween, etc.
2. *Historical*—Usually overworked, but you might try it again: the origin of Valentine's Day, the many New Year's celebrations.
3. *Universality*—How do others celebrate Easter or their own equivalent of the Fourth of July?
4. *Changes*—Compare today's Halloween with the past.
5. *New* ways to celebrate.
6. *New* gifts appropriate to the holiday.
7. *New* locales at which to celebrate the holiday; precisely why I took travel writers to London one Christmas, to see how the English celebrate—and write about it!

Starter lines

Sometimes super ideas occur when you provide starter lines, the answer to which is the heart of the article. Let me suggest six that work well for me:

1. *What if* (to which I might add) we paid people for good ideas? *What if* we used birth control as a criterion for foreign aid?
2. *What about* developing a computer that will convert tape cassettes—better yet, ideas—into printouts?
3. *What ever happened to* (name anybody in any field currently

out of public view)?

4. *Why can't we* convert water into gasoline?

5. *What would happen if* we ran out of fossil fuels tomorrow?

6. *How did* Lassie find her way home 1,000 untrammeled miles? *How did* I think up so many goofy examples?

Begin with the opening question, complete it in an interrogatory way, and by providing the answer, you have found the heart of the article.

This process isn't quite as odd as it may appear, since most professionals quickly convert subjects into questions and use the replies, in their developmental stages, as the outlines for their articles. We are simply starting with the question here, shortcutting the process.

You can apply these—or similar leading questions—to almost any topic and at least emerge with stimulating ideas that can then be tested for article applicability.

Look at your own day

Another excellent source of ideas is your average day. If, for one day, you could keep a list of all your thoughts, worries, dreams, suspicions, fears, even activities, you'd have a list ripe for a year's worth of sales.

You awake at 7 but lay there until 7:30. The article is called "The Early Morning Blues, or How Do You Kick Yourself Out of Bed?"

You cycle every morning, or most mornings. Others have their own life-extending peculiarities. A score of stories could be written about those activities, sports, hobbies.

Do you ever wonder why there are so many different razors and blades? Are they really any different? Which are best? Why do they change so often? "The Great Blade Rip-Off" I'd call it. (Extend that to toothpaste, shaving gels or deodorants.)

Some communities have organized citizen patrols to keep the area safe. How are they working? How common is the practice? How did it start? Here is a story that would have eager readership countrywide.

You work. Every job is a hotbed of articles.

After work, you go to a movie, buy popcorn, and perhaps pizza later. Food grossly overpriced. Popcorn, $.26 of value sold for $2.50 or more. Pizza is worse. The articles are called "The Great Popcorn

Robbery" or "The Pizza Purloinment." Such consumer-related stories sell well.

On your way home, you notice an all-night hot dog stand. You talk with the Cuban couple who run it. They've never been robbed. They love the work. They came to America to set up their own business and work together. Readers love success stories.

Climbing into bed, you wonder, for the tenth time, if you really could learn Spanish while listening to a tape while you slept. Sleeping is a subject that never tires the reader. And doing something positive while sawing *z's* is a natural.

What have I done? Skipped through a hypothetical day and pointed at everyday activities and occurrences that others might want to know about. I didn't have to travel or dip into history books or read the horoscope to find ideas: I just opened my eyes, looked at what I've been seeing for days or years and asked which of those things others would also like to know about.

Yet a footnote is necessary. When I actually write these ideas into articles *I* disappear. The "early morning blues" aren't mine, but everybody's. I research "depression at dawn," investigate procrastination, ask how much of my slow start is due to the lingering aftereffects of deep sleep and so on. My observations are universalized. Remember, people want to read about themselves, as they are, might be or would be but for the grace of God. As with most articles, while the curiosity is mine, the tale is told third person.

Travel topics

For the appendix of a travel-writing book I wrote a few years back, I created a list of 365 travel article ideas, in title form. It was far easier than I imagined finding the ready-to-use topics.

One technique was to take any human-based subject and tell how it is in a different setting—the greater the difference, usually the greater the interest.

Some years back I recall being surprised when I first saw an escalator in a two-story "department store" in Salvador (locally called Bahia), Brazil. Still, an article about an escalator in U.S. publications wouldn't catch much interest unless it was plunk in the middle of a jungle or desert. But when I entered that same store weeks later, I found at least five hundred people clustered around the "rolling stairs," gaping. It seems that two aborigines, young men, had been brought to the city as part of a linguistic study. They had never left the jungle before. Wearing loincloths and brightly feathered headgear, barefoot and firmly gripping tufted spears, the teenage lads took turns jabbing at the stairs and letting out excited shouts, then running up a few feet and leaping back to the ground. Every time they landed safely, the crowd cheered and clapped! I have no idea how this ended. They were still poking, shouting and leaping twenty minutes later when I had to leave. It only occurred to me a decade hence that I should have stayed and spoken to the guides who were accompanying the bewildered, animated natives, to write a full account of how they had found and confronted civilization, topping it off with an interview, through a translator, with the Indians themselves.

The point is that almost anything is fair game for a selling article if its distance in mileage or cultural time is sufficient to provoke readership curiosity. I had found a sure-selling escalator story!

Even small differences can lead to selling copy. Quilting magazines want to know about patterns, material and marketing, be it from Idaho, Ireland or the Isle of Mu. Local cures of Bali flatulence, why one doesn't wink at maidens in rural Burma and how ceremonial pots are fired in Bolivia are the stuff of selling articles.

So an important thing any topic-seeking travel writer might do would be to reread and apply any of the eight topic-provoking steps just explained from the vantage point of each new locale or culture.

Look closely at everyday life at the new site and report about it in an appropriate U.S. publication. Consider infants, youngsters, teens, honeymooners and retirees—from that culture or as it applies to visiting Americans—as the core of enlightening, exciting, probably amusing pieces. Tie in newspaper accounts of what is happening in other places with a greater explanation of why that is occurring and what it portends for the future, ours and theirs. Relate travel pieces to significant dates, anniversaries or seasons there or in the U.S. Explain holidays celebrated elsewhere, or how American holidays are observed, viewed or avoided in other places. Apply the "starting questions" to foreign cultures. Trace an "average day" for folks there at different social levels.

Then add to that huge pit of potential topics those subjects that are directly related to travel itself.

What immediately confronts the would-be traveler?

1. *Where should you go?* How do you select "perfect" travel destinations? How do you determine the best blend of activities when you arrive? How do you create a trip to favorite old places and exciting new sites?

2. *How do you get there?* Is the "getting there" as important as the arriving, so a sea cruise would make more sense than the fastest jet? Do you want to go there directly, or should stops to and fro be included? Should you seek out the international airlines with non-smoking flights?

3. *How can you keep the travel costs down?* What is the best deal your travel agent can offer? Should you buy a ticket from a "bucket shop"? Could you be an air courier? Are there budget hotels or low-cost tours?

4. *Should you go alone or team up with others?* Again, are group tours an option? Could you meet others at the destination, leaving you with greater single-travel flexibility both coming and going? Should you seek a companion among your friends before making travel commitments?

You get the idea. You make a list of every concern you face, or could, in setting up a trip, frame each concern as a question, then create articles from potential responses. If you are facing that problem, so are other travelers. Voilá, an article in print—and money to feed your other travel vices!

Let your mind wander to see the many fields where such questions/answers/articles lie, at every phase of trip conceptualization and planning: ticket purchase, supply and equipment provision, comfort and amusement during the trip itself, logistics at every step of the journey, money needed and how it can be obtained at the destination, caution and security, what foods to try and which to avoid, proper attire en route and there, what there is to do at the key sites, how to avoid or overcome loneliness, how to infuse more joy or love or awe at every step, how to return refreshed from an exacting vacation. Those are the things that travel editors need, readers read and too few writers even consider. If written with humor and enthusiasm, plus fresh insights and practical tips, how can you be denied copy space?

Start with one broad premise: Travelers are just you and me going somewhere else for a variety of reasons who want to reap everything positive immediately and in abundance—fun, excitement, rest, wonderment, love, relaxation and unforgettable memories—without hassles, inexpensively and with a minimum of lifting.

Tell them how to do that. And also paint true yet heart-stopping visions of the places they want to visit. All-you-ever-wanted-to-know, definitive destination articles that leap off the page but remain accurate when seen in person.

One way to know what travel readers want to read, and how it must be written, is to see what they are reading now. Spend a week studying what appears on the pages where you want to be published. Then either give them more of the same, but better, or see what hasn't been said, then write it at that same high level. (Chapter four provides more information about researching travel topics.)

Research

Now that you have an action plan and an idea for a magazine article, you can either make things up or you can research the topic. While the first lies in the fiction domain, editors using nonfiction prefer the second. This chapter should help.

Research for query letters

If the editor expects to be queried, as most magazine and book editors do, your research obligations will be far less than for an editor who expects to receive the entire manuscript, as would most newspaper editors.

A query letter is usually one page long for articles, and two, with attachments, for books. So you must complete enough research to fill the page or pages, then convert your findings into accurate, arresting copy. You must also know, as a result of that research, that what you are promising in the query you can later provide as an article or book, should the response be affirmative.

Most query letters require several hours to research, write and mail. If the response is positive and the resulting manuscript is about the subject promised, written to the level of the publication, your chance of a sale is excellent, far better than 50 percent, closer to 90 percent. You will have to complete your detailed research later, but it will be limited by the needs of the editor, which you can readily study in recent purchases by that editor. In other words, this means a few hours of research now on a gamble against a likely, higher paying buy later.

After all, the query letter simply asks, "Would you be interested in buying an article or book about _____?" You only do the final research and write the text after you know the editor is indeed interested and you can study what he has recently bought so you know the kind of research and writing needed.

Research for direct, simultaneous submissions

A full manuscript requires all of the research up front, checked and double-checked, presented in the proper format, with the source of any point challenged readily available at the editor's request.

The difference between research for a query and a full, direct submission is volume and depth.

The financial difference is greater—as is the gamble.

Direct submissions are far riskier and usually pay much less. If they must be pursued one at a time, they simply are not worth the time and effort required unless you can find markets where you can simultaneously submit the same completed copy to many publications. Five categories usually accept simultaneous submissions: newspapers, newspaper weekly magazines (usually operated somewhat autonomously from the newspaper itself), regional publications, religious publications and in-flight magazines.

All want simultaneously submitted material sent in final form: completely researched, written and illustrated (if appropriate), with a cover note. Nobody is aware of the submission before it arrives, space has not been saved for it and you have no way of judging who would be the most favorable receiver or when would be the best time to get it.

Nor do you have any way to form-fit your prose to any one publication. Rather you will write an article for, say, a dozen newspaper travel sections, keep the specifics broad enough to be usable in all locales and send it off.

It takes longer to prepare a final manuscript than a query (though the hours can be divided by the number of publications purchasing it for a better time-energy comparison), the buyers often pay much less (usually a third to a half) than those expecting queries and the chances of it being bought unsolicited are also far lower.

Thus unsolicited manuscripts, totally researched and written, are a gamble. But, if sent to simultaneous submission editors where you can sell them to many publications at the same time, they can be worth pursuing.

Which brings us to the actual research itself. Whether it is done in two major installments, as with query letters, or one extended push, to write a direct submission, the same path is ultimately taken.

The process and sources of research

Articles are composed of facts, quotes and anecdotes. Add the artwork sometimes required—photos, line drawings, maps, charts—and you have all you will need to thrive by selling your writing.

Finding those base elements couldn't be easier. Libraries and life itself surround us with facts, quotes and anecdotes from the past and present.

What's harder is finding the specific ones required to make an idea, then an article, bristle with interest, accuracy and verve. Just as important is spending the least amount of time finding the most productive material that will bring you the best return, or at least get you in print the most often.

Articles almost always need at least two of the three, but you must divine the necessary combination and in what ratio they are preferred, since that will tell you where to aim your research.

For example, scientific articles are heavily factual with some quotations to establish authority. Most historical pieces in popular magazines are factual and anecdotal, often with quotes. Hollywood gossip-type articles are usually anecdotal, with many quotes—and alarmingly few facts.

Beyond those three components, another important element distinguishes the kinds of articles bought: the degree of humor used. Some use straight humor, as in *Mad*; some are humorous, in that the style is humorous but there is an informative purpose to the article; and some avoid humor as though it were evil and infectious. But here let's focus on the facts, quotes and anecdotes.

As types of writing have different ratios of the three key components and the amount and kind of humor used, so do publications. The blend of those often provides the only true "fingerprint" or "copyprint" distinguishing one publication from another. Some call that style!

Assuming you have read some recent issues of the magazine for which you are about to write and have a sense of how it uses facts, quotes, anecdotes and humor, you should know what you should seek in which proportion.

Let's concentrate on where to find the written material first, then how to find and use spoken material, and finally how to draw out or create material that has yet to be written or interviewed.

First, let's reiterate the two most important time-savers in article research:

1. You must start by clearly defining the article's subject or theme before you research it. Research is infinitely faster if you know what you're looking for.

2. You must know how the article will be submitted so you know when you need to do the research. Will you query first, with quick research up front and the bulk of it to follow, or will you submit the full, researched article at the outset?

When you have a subject in mind and know the proper research sequence, you must find the resources.

Facts and the library

Much of your background or preparation work will come from the library—or directly to you through your computer from a printed source.

It's a huge blessing if you are fortunate enough to live within driving distance of a good college or university library. Even a city library is valuable, particularly if you need to look through the more commercial magazines, since those are less frequently found in academic depositories. The most important thing, though, is that your library have a good, current, accessible reference section, and hopefully a well-trained reference librarian, "the angel of the stacks."

Except for the reference material, almost anything else you need can be secured from other libraries through Interlibrary Loan, an inexpensive and usually fast process whereby books are exchanged. Ask your librarian about the costs and other details, plus how you can find what is available at other libraries without having to travel to them first.

(Here your computer can be extremely valuable, using the Internet to ferret out your specific reference listings nationwide.)

Let's assume your library is average or better in its holdings. More than just the rows of fiction and nonfiction books, it has current and past issues of periodicals and newspapers and a wide assortment of reference texts (such as dictionaries, encyclopedias, bibliographies, indexes to magazines, annuals, handbooks, biographical and historical dictionaries, maps, atlases and much more). Usually a library has a vertical file much loved by travel writers for the pamphlets and maps it contains. And a surprising number of libraries have audiovisual material you can use there or take home that include microfilm, microfiche, slides, pictures, recordings, movie films, videos and more.

One thing is certain: If you do much writing at all, you will soon need virtually every service your library offers. It's better to know of each one's existence and location at the outset than to have to reinvent the wheel—or the facts—each time because of your ignorance.

A perspective on the currency of available resources helps you select the best ones.

If you want to know up-to-the-minute facts about your topic, be forewarned that you won't find them in books. You will get depth, breadth, perspective and illustration in a book, but not newness. Most books have been in the writing, editing, printing, binding and distributing process for at least six months (more likely eighteen) before they appear on the library shelf. So what passes for new is often from six months to several years old.

If your subject is glacial retreat, that might be fine; but if it's the latest word in microcomputers, six months might as well be six eons.

More current will be magazine material. If the magazine is a weekly, such as *Time, Newsweek* or the *U.S. News and World Report,* its material might be less than twenty-four hours old. If it comes from a monthly commercial magazine, the typical lead time is two to three months, which means that the copy is that old when you read it fresh from the rack. Academic journals are generally far more dated, many eight months to a year behind.

Newspapers contain the most current paper-print material. You've seen news sitcoms on TV or their equivalent at the movies: "Stop-the-press!" scoops are sometimes inserted as fast as the material can be set. It's a few minutes old when it hits the streets. Yet with that blessing comes a bane: The content might be 100 percent new but it might also be full of errors. The point is clear. The faster the facts have been rushed to print, the greater the risk of their being inaccurate.

Even quicker is the on-the-spot TV, radio or Internet report of a fast-breaking news item. But that too is suspect concerning accuracy. It is filtered by the choice of location, what the newscaster knows, the questions asked or sites shown and the reliability of those spoken to.

There's another quick way to get facts: Contacting the person involved and directly ask her what you want to know. That's often the fastest and most effective means of all, but it can also be the most wildly inaccurate.

My point here is that all items in the library, or used as live sources, must be considered from two levels: their timeliness and their reliability. The fresher the fact, the more you must double-check that accuracy, then probably check it once again!

Newspapers

Let's start with the newspapers in your library. Some are national and have excellent reputations for in-depth analyses on a hemispheric scale, for example, *The New York Times*, *The Christian Science Monitor* and *The Wall Street Journal*. Others are very detailed about your city or county.

To see what has appeared about your topic on their pages, check the respective newspaper indexes, or visit the "morgue" at the local newspaper office. *The New York Times* has a comprehensive index and is usually available on microfilm, as one can often also find the *Chicago Tribune* and the *Los Angeles Times*. See if the library has the computerized National Newspaper Index, or an equivalent, and if the major dailies nearby are indexed at your library. You can use these indexes either to find related material or as a historical backdrop. (During the bicentennial, when I wrote a series of articles about 1876, I began by checking the 1876 *The New York Times Index* and noted all of the names and events I knew or wanted to know more about, then read the related articles and books.)

Don't be surprised to find the exact same article or wording in a couple of newspapers since much of their content comes from the wire services, such as the Associated Press or the UPI. In those cases, pay particular attention to the additional material each paper has added either to that article or to a nearby related article or sidebar with a local tie-in.

Once you have compiled the best references, find the actual articles on microfilm or from the Internet (see "Using Your Computer" at the end of this chapter for more information) and extract what you need from them. Checking the major articles in each issue sometimes provides a valuable time set into which you can place the information you are extracting.

Magazines

Magazines are our next category. They are also called periodicals or serials. The terms are worth defining.

"Magazine" really means storehouse or collection, and some commercial magazines you will write for are just that, a collection of unrelated articles about a variety of topics. The definition of magazine has been extended by common usage to include the many special interest or single-subject publications that exist to serve their highly defined buying niches. A magazine for model airplane builders, petunia growers, wrestling fans. These include virtually all trades, professions, hobbies and sports. Most of today's magazines fall in this latter category.

"Periodicals" means that they are published periodically, usually at stated intervals (or "serially"), so magazines also fit in this category. You can find the most complete list of periodicals in *Ulrich's International Periodicals Directory*. It lists 120,000 from more than 61,000 publishers in 197 countries!

It would be temporally imprudent to leaf through that many periodicals to find information about your topic or to locate similar publications. Periodical indexes save the day!

Over the years the most widely used has been the commercial magazine guide for the U.S., the *Readers' Guide to Periodical Literature*, simply called the *Readers' Guide*. I've yet to find a library without it, though you must check its index to be certain the specific publication you want to know about is listed. As libraries convert their holdings to computer access, find the equivalent to the *Readers' Guide* on computer. A widely found version is InfoTrac's Magazine Index Plus.

There are several dozen more indexes that are valuable time-savers. One you will want to consult quickly is the *Bibliographic Index*, to see who else has put together a bibliography about your topic. If the bibliography is extensive, that alone could save you hours. Then there are the indexes by academic subject. You will find them for articles in agriculture, biology, business, education, engineering, nursing, etc. Or by religion or vocation; there are indexes to poetry, to library resources, to essays. Let your reference librarian explain this bonanza.

Encyclopedias and dictionaries

I've spoken of newspapers and periodicals because that's where you find the most recent facts. But you should also consider using an encyclopedia as a starting point for your research, despite the fact that teachers and editors told or tell you not to give them a reworked robbery from the *Britannica*.

Why the encyclopedia? Because what you must know when dealing with a topic is the whole of the subject given concisely and accurately so you fully understand the historical background and current position of the smaller segment of it that you will write about. In reading the encyclopedia, you will find hard facts as well as related terms you can use for cross-referencing when you later use the card catalog. Most encyclopedias also have short bibliographies you may want to use, and some even have annuals that bring topics up to date.

You may also want to take a quick look at your topic in the dictionary to be sure you understand its exact meaning, even how the words came into use or being. Both the encyclopedia and dictionary will give you substance against which to test the accuracy of subsequent material. Don't forget: When all is researched and written, it is accuracy— or the lack of it—that will be longest remembered.

Bibliographies and booklets

Once you have a topic clearly in mind, the best way to use a library is to work from the general to the specific, from an overview to the precise facts required.

We spoke of starting with the encyclopedia and dictionary, for factual and linguistic bases. My next stop would be to look over the bibliographies and book lists, if my subject were large and from it I expected to develop several or many articles.

To clarify the terms, both are book lists, but a bibliography generally means a larger, more inclusive listing, sometimes everything known to have been published on the subject or to have been written by an author.

Earlier I mentioned the *Bibliographic Index* when discussing periodicals. That is usually your best first source for bibliographies. You can also use Besterman's *A World Bibliography of Bibliographies*.

If you want to know what books are currently in print about a topic, there are two key sources available at almost all libraries. For a world list of books published in English, there is the *CBI*, or *Cumulative Book Index*. For books printed in the U.S., you will want to see a current *Books in Print*. The latter has a companion that expedites your job even more, called the *Subject Guide to Books in Print*.

Incidentally, if you're thinking of writing a book in the near future, to see if somebody is about to spring the same gem on the reading public, check *Forthcoming Books* to find out what is expected to be printed in the next six months.

There are also book digests and book review publications if you wish to appraise the sources. Ask your librarian about these.

Indexes, card catalogs, microfiche, microfilm and dissertations

At this point you have an overview and a list of books that seem to hit your topic head-on. Now is when I would consult the newspaper and periodical indexes such as *The New York Times Index* and the *Readers' Guide to Periodical Literature*, or the academic counterparts I mentioned earlier. The purpose is to again identify those specific articles needed to give you facts, printed quotes and anecdotes.

Inevitably, and in your case now, you will be drawn to the famous, or infamous, card catalog, which, incidentally, may have given way to microfilm, which contains the same information but is harder to read, or a computer database.

There are two ways the library lists the cards: by author and by title. If you have a list of bibliographical sources, try the authors first, the subject second. Approaching a topic from both angles will obviously yield greater rewards.

You're surely familiar with card catalogs, so I'll simply remind you that the card, microfilm or database will at least list the author, book, date of publication, occasionally a line or two about the book's contents and the call number. These numbers will adhere either to the Dewey Decimal or the Library of Congress System, which is unimportant here: You must simply jot down the information, then find the number on the stacks. That final process is known as cruising the stacks!

Often a reward awaits you on the shelves: many more books about the same topic that you didn't see in the card catalog. So plan to browse during your stack search, visiting each area numbered on the various listings.

There is something else the card catalog will reveal that can prove extraordinarily valuable: the existence of material on microfilm or microfiche.

Let me give you an example of the second. I was preparing some articles about the year 1876 a year or so before the bicentennial, as I said earlier, and I wanted some firsthand anecdotal material about the Wild West. Lo and behold, at a state university library in California, the cards mentioned two altogether different items on microfiche that proved to be the diamonds that made the pieces sparkle.

One was a diary kept by an Illinois lad who headed west, went to Cheyenne and from there overland to Deadwood to pan for gold. Not only did he leave a misspelled account of his activities on July 4, 1876, he told of "Wild Bill" Hickok being shot while playing poker, and much more.

At the same time, I was able to read two full guidebooks to the Centennial Exhibition in Philadelphia, where Alexander Graham Bell first displayed the telephone, linoleum was introduced, the King of Brazil officiated and the man who shot John Wilkes Booth was a guard. One of the guidebooks was 700-plus pages and was preserved on one piece of hard plastic about $3'' \times 5''$, which are microfiches.

Librarians will show you how to use microfiche and microfilm. Be aware of their existence and the wealth of material, mostly historical, they contain.

Sometimes doctoral dissertations have been written about your topic. They too will be listed, usually, in the card catalogs. They are also frequently found on microfilm or microfiche. There are particular references to dissertations that should be consulted, to be able to include directed research in your articles.

Other library sources

Don't forget the possibility that the books you find on the stacks will have their own bibliographies. Often a book of limited use will prove to be far more valuable because it gives sources you haven't found or considered. So always flip to the table of contents or back section of every reputable reference to see what it used as source material. Let an earlier author do much of your hunting for you.

Let's talk about some lesser known books, or types of books, you will find at the library that can add depth or can simplify your tasks.

I like Alden Todd's *Finding Facts Fast*. My newspaper friends use this to save time, and I do too. More scholarly but also useful is Margaret G. Cook's *The New Library Key*. She is particularly good in describing reference books.

There are a half-dozen books I call the "date books" because they will take any historical date and put it into perspective. There is the *Dictionary of Dates*, the *Book of Dates*, *The Timetables of History*, etc. My favorite is fairly new and super reading about years past, called *The People's Chronology*, by James Trager. As mentioned earlier, many of the encyclopedias have annuals that will provide you with detailed descriptions of events that took place during that year.

In the library's reference section you will find a row of books with or about quotations as well as books about etiquette, flags, nicknames, legends and coats of arms. *Famous First Facts* and *Facts on File* deserve a look, and never forget the wealth of information in the U.S. Government data section, particularly census data and related abstracts.

I mentioned quotation books in passing but here we should focus on them at some depth since quotes are a valuable component of selling copy. Printed quotes tend to be historic in nature, but some will be fairly recent—age is often less crucial than finding the proper phrase well turned.

Bergen Evans's *Dictionary of Quotations* is the most fun to read, Rhoda Thomas Tripp's *The International Thesaurus of Quotations* has some of the oddest and Adams's *The Home Book of Humorous Quotations* will make you laugh, sometimes. Look these over yourself to find that one telling phrase or catchy lead that will help put your piece in print.

Getting live quotes from equally live people, and anecdotes in person, is important. Here the biographical dictionaries play a key role. The most useful are the *Current Biography*, a monthly updating on people now prominent, from media figures to scientists and statesmen, and *The New York Times Biographical Edition*, a weekly update your library may have. For congresspeople, find the *Official Congressional Directory*, with a new edition each session. There are many, many *Who's Whos*, by country, by profession, by sex, etc. Plus the *Dictionary of American Biography* for those who were living and famous.

There is much more I could say about the library as an e'er bubbling fountain of background material, but let's talk now about living sources, then about how to create other material later. In closing our library segment, let me remind you one last time that *Finding Facts Fast* and reference librarians, eager to serve, will be loving guides through the labyrinths of the library.

Live interviews

Getting live interviews is far easier than you imagine, but it requires some sleuthing and some preparation on your part. I'm not going into the full process of interviewing here, for our purpose is to find the sources, but let me touch lightly on the first phases of interviewing because that starts with finding a person to interview, then setting up the actual exchange.

The easiest way to find starter names for interviews is to see with whom other writers spoke when writing about the same or a similar subject. If the person they interviewed is "the" expert, that's who you should speak with as well. Or if those interviewed came from a larger group, go to others within that group. For example, if you are writing about the "slurve," the fairly new pitch in baseball, which is a combination slider and curve, and you've seen one pitcher interviewed about it, find another pitcher who throws it and interview both!

Sometimes the article takes both sides of an issue, say, the pro- and anti-abortion viewpoints. You know who the spokesperson for the pro-abortion or pro-choice group is but have no idea about the opposition. Ask the person you speak with from the pro- side. Better than anybody that person will know the opposition, and 90 percent of the time will share the name with you.

Other times you have a super subject and simply no idea where to begin. Find the academic field closest to that topic and ask a venerable professor at a nearby university to help get you started. Or if it concerns a product, go to the firm or trade association closest to it: Someone there will point you in the right direction. Newspaper writers are very helpful. City desk types who have rubbed elbows with every kind of creature can usually set you off to the right pasture. And even the reference librarians can offer solid suggestions, though they may be blissfully ignorant of the follow-up interview process.

Beginners often wilt at the thought of talking to "big names" or "famous people." True, some folks with fame are hard to reach or get to talk. The hardest, I've found, are academics, who are extremely suspicious of whatever you are doing, and lower echelon business executives, who are afraid to say hello for fear it's a trade secret and will put their jobs in jeopardy.

Yet most people, if approached correctly, will gladly speak with you for a few minutes, and some for longer. Most interviews last at most fifteen minutes, so that's fine. It simply forces you to organize well in advance and limit your questions to the absolute essentials needed to produce a solid article.

I've spoken with presidents in South America, ambassadors, politicians of all stripes in the U.S., movie stars, sports personalities, academics, businessfolk and plenty of people just like us, and hardly a one said no or failed to give me enough to significantly add to my article. What made it simple was the preparation before I ever contacted them.

For starters, I knew precisely what the article would be about, so I had one or a couple specific questions I had to ask. Second, I knew the interviewee was the person whose reply I needed to produce the strongest article possible. Third, I knew enough about the individual that I didn't have to spend fifteen minutes building the biographical facts that were available elsewhere.

So let's talk about what you should know about the person before you arrange the interview. You must know how to spell and pronounce her name, the current position she holds, why she is qualified to answer your questions and how her position concerning the issue relates to others' positions. Finally, you should know how to get in touch with the person.

Where do you find all of this? Much of it from other interviews with that person, from her affiliations with groups whose position or stand you know, from her writings or speeches. If she works for a company or an institution, see if this group has a public relations office that will send you biographical and other material. If she is an entertainer or such, contact her agent. If she appears in *Current Biography* or a *Who's Who* . . . or has been the subject of an article in a major newspaper or magazine, we've already spoken of how you find that information.

When a person's fame, as it is, is spread but locally, check with the town newspaper to see what it can offer. Some papers will let you see their clippings or morgue material; at others, the editor is the entire filing system, and he will give you a few fingers of prose about the person in question, plus a name or two of locals who might provide more information.

The last step prior to holding the interview is to determine where the article will appear. If you follow the professional system, you did that long ago, and the interview comes after a go-ahead from an interested publication, so when the person asks who you are writing for, as most interview subjects do, you have a name.

But if you are just taking your chances and writing a piece in the hope that some editor will buy it, the worst thing you can reply is, "I don't know." The second worst is that you are a freelancer or, God forbid, a journalism student completing an assignment. (The more professional your interviewee, the less likely she will have time for a blind interview.) So the least you'd better have at hand is the name of a publication that would likely use your piece—and hope the person doesn't probe too deeply.

Beyond this point we are at the interviewing stage, and that is beyond the scope of this book. An excellent text is Michael Schumacher's *Creative Conversatons: The Writer's Guide to Conducting Interviews*.

One final comment about finding quotation sources, though: When you are interviewing a person and he mentions a subject or facet you want to explore more fully, ask him who he knows who could provide some additional depth about those points.

Anecdotes

Anecdotes are short, entertaining accounts of some happening, usually personal or biographical. These can come from written material or can emanate from a live interview. We've discussed how to find the sources for each, so all I must do here is emphasize that anecdotes are often the best way to prove points, show a person in action or add some human depth to pieces that would die bloodless without them. They should be looked for and asked about.

Sports articles are the best examples I can think of that show how crucial an anecdote is to putting flesh on people and situations. They bring a sense of actuality, of immediacy, of vitality to facts and quotes. In short, while at the library or interviewing actively, seek the telling tales.

Creating your own information

Once in my jaded past I helped promote a multimedia kit about dying and death. We needed some graphic slides of funeral customs around the world, plus information about the customs from the provider. Photo agencies wouldn't do. So I ran an ad in a newspaper in Wheaton, Illinois, site of a fundamentalist college and many returned missionaries. One ad brought several hundred slides from every corner of humanity. We had twice as many excellent items as we could use.

I read about an author who needed information for a book about the man's side of divorce who found his material by running an ad that said, "Divorced men: serious author seeks interviews with men hurt by divorce." He got twenty-five responses!

And George Plimpton needed firsthand accounts for a book of the funeral train carrying Robert Kennedy's body. He ran ads in the towns through which the train passed, and got what he needed.

A bit of advice here: Keep your ads direct, strong and clear, and if you're female, it's best to use your initial rather than your first name. You may want to list a phone number or P.O. box if you want anonymity until you've screened out the respondents.

Once they do call, be straightforward and businesslike, since people are naturally suspicious. Win their trust, then make it easy for them by interviewing on the phone or going to them. You needn't pay unless their response requires them to incur costs or spend much time, like having to travel somewhere to undergo extensive testing, etc. People are glad to help, and the fact that their names may appear in print is usually payment enough.

Using your computer

Since I grew up journalistically in the byteless precomputer era, the techniques so far described have been library based and have mostly required taking notes and wandering through the stacks.

Electricity and chips to the rescue! Card catalogs are now computerized in the library, listings can often be printed as they are found, the *Readers' Guide to Periodical Literature* has yielded to the computerized Magazine Index Plus, or an equivalent. Reviews of articles cited can as often be read on a monitor, even printed out, to see if it's even worth the effort of reading the entire original.

If you are linked from your modemized home computers to online services (such as CompuServe or America Online), you can travel much farther faster without leaving your office or den. You can call up the actual articles, printing out what you need. You can peruse entire encyclopedias, find historical maps, even paperchat directly with folks worldwide through e-mail and the Internet.

Further, while it's still finding legs and form, through the Internet you can read about the subways of the world, Amtrack schedules, a hitchhiker's guide to New York City, the addresses of all U.S. consulates worldwide, even the global details about accommodations wanted to buy, rent, swap and sell.

Books will show you how to use online services to expedite your research: Peter Rutten's *Net Guide: Your Map to the Services, Information and Entertainment on the Electronic Highway* and Charles Bowen's *CompuServe From A to Z* are two examples.

CompuServe's own literature directs you to two references through which you can search the airline reservation systems for the lowest fares on all major domestic and international airlines, then make your own reservations. Plus you can access detailed restaurant guides, golf courses and hotels. You can also check the daily U.S. Department of State Advisories to see where not to go, plus visa advisories about what you need for entry into other countries.

Alas, computers are simply new tools to research quicker or more conveniently. You still need the facts, quotes and anecdotes or what you write won't sell.

Travel research sources

So much for general research tools, with an occasional travel application. Almost any aspect of specialized writing has sources peculiar to it. Let's focus more tightly on travel writing research in the section that follows, both since more writers will at least dabble in travel than any other focus and as an example of how one might search for other, nontravel categories for parallel sources and offerings.

Travel writers need to know four things: how to find what their buyers need; more about the country; how to get there; and what to see and do once they arrive.

How to find what the buyers need

There are two ways to provide article ideas to travel magazine editors that have a good chance of being requested from a query and then bought.

One is to begin with the idea, research it fully to see what there is about it that the magazine's readers would find irresistible, impart that in a sparkling query letter, then write the desired article in the same fine fashion.

The other suggests that you study the target publication in painful detail, fathom out what it uses and what it needs and find those topics to fill its gaps.

You must become familiar with travel magazines. Which in turn means a schmooze with *Writer's Market*, some hours in the current periodicals section of your library and a further look at the magazine section of the news rack or supermarket.

Some target markets are obvious: *Condé Nast Traveler, Adventure West, Travel Holiday, Travel and Leisure*. Almost all consumer magazines use travel: women's, men's, automobile, RV, camping, skiing, sailing, even running.

Some aren't so obvious: all the rest. Any article that requires going from here to there qualifies. "Fossil hunting" is travel if you must go somewhere to do it. So you find the specialty publications sought by fossil hunters, paper-pitch the peculiar virtues of your selected article site to one of those editors, get the query nod, go and dig, and your income is no less a travel reward than "All You Ever Wanted to Know About Ciudad del Este, Paraguay!"

Finding out more about the country

Once you have a site in mind, you need both general and specific information about the locale.

Some of that is nearby; some requires letters or phone calls to bring it to you.

In the library or through a computer online link, you can find encyclopedias and both magazine and newspaper articles used in, say, the past ten years. See if there is a Time-Life book about the topic. Comb the shelves in the larger bookstores or in the travel boutique stores. Ask your travel agent for brochures or flyers. See if the airlines have anything to distribute. Read the broader books about the regions, such as *The Central American Fact Book*, *England on $60 a Day* or the *Maverick Guide to Hawaii*. Check the guidebooks to see what new information they contain, from firms or names such as Frommer, Fodor, Waldo, Fielding and Baedeker.

If your library doesn't have it, get the most recent country book in the Area Handbook Series, titled *Greece* (insert your country): *A Country Study*, from the Superintendent of Documents, U.S. Government Publishing Office, Washington, DC 20402. They are excellent. If your destination is in the U.S., see what else the federal government has in print and available at little or no cost by consulting the *Guide to Federal Publications: Consumer Information of the U.S. Travel Services* (U.S. Department of Commerce, Washington, DC 20230)— check the government documents section of your library first. Don't forget the states, either. A letter to the Tourism Department of the state government explaining your needs often yields exciting results.

If your destination is abroad, ask the tourist office of that country to send you all available information plus a map. (Find those offices through the phone books of the major cities, that country's consulates or its Washington, DC, embassy.)

Don't forget travel trade shows in major cities. Handouts abound, often distributed by folks who can give specific details. Contact the convention bureau or your local travel agent for dates and how to get admitted.

How to get there

Once you have a general idea about your target area, how can you get there quickly and inexpensively? Better yet, how can you add in extra writing sites coming and going at little or no additional travel cost?

It's almost too easy if you're driving. Get a map (at the service station, library or through an auto club), study the routes to and from, scour your information sources and plot the path.

If you're flying, either use your travel agent (seeing what layovers are possible without additional cost) or check the back (or travel) pages of your newspaper (Sunday is best) for consolidators who sell at heavily discounted rates.

The best book around for almost all travel discounts is Suzanne Hogsett's *Bargain Travel Resource Book*. (Contact Travel Easy, 3427 Thomas Drive, Palo Alto, CA 94303.)

Don't forget the possibility of being an air courier, which can save you 50 to 85 percent on your overseas rates on specific European, Asian and South American routes. Hogsett gives full details, and a chapter in my latest book, *The Travel Writer's Guide*, also explains the process.

What to see and do once you arrive

I presume that by this point you have studied other books, articles and pamphlets about your destination site and know what other writers wrote about and thought was worth seeing.

From that you may have selected a particular location and built your query promise around it. If so, and you received a go-ahead, that must be the object of most of your attention. But you will want to visit the other local places worth comment too, to add to the article in question or to prepare a broader site piece to sell to newspapers or to magazines when you return, after querying.

The first thing you must do, upon arriving, is contact the key people you wish to interview. Make a specific appointment with each, then use the time around the interviews to observe, photo and speak with others. Double-check the facts you bring with you: Are they current, accurate, full? What more do you need to know?

Ask locals what they know about the places you are visiting. Anything unusual happen(ing) there? Any superstitions about it? Any historical or folklore? Also ask them what else is interesting there or nearby that is less known to outsiders. What do *they* do for fun? Where do they go? What events or festivals are celebrated there? When? What are they like?

Often you can find excellent local booklets or books about the site. Check them closely, and buy what you need. Perhaps the author lives there: Who better to interview? Buy town or regional maps too.

Keep your eye open for those photos that capture in one shot the site, mood and sense of the place. Seek a blend of all-encompassing, single-facet and up-close photos in both color (slides) and black and white. Remember that the same shot at dawn, noon and dusk may be remarkably different, so consider the other hours as well for the best photos. Also, most publications want people doing related things in most photos.

Determine when you get there the kinds of information you need to make the article "work," then try to get even more. Note each article's needs on the outside of a respective folder, then cross off each need as you gather the info. Work every day, but also take time to have fun, wander around, gawk. Just keep your cameras at hand in case those key photo opportunities pop up.

The trick is to focus fully on the article object when you are working on it, and keep it in mind during the off hours in case something else appears or is said that can be added to it. A notebook in the pocket is ideal to capture those observations or comments.

When you're done at that site, either move on to another or hunker in for rest and relaxation!

With research, what takes you many hours to do the first time will take many minutes later. It gets easier and the results are better. I implied it earlier but it bears stating: What lingers longest in writing are the errors, the facts that aren't, the misquotes, the telling anecdotes that never took place. You can't afford any of those if you want to earn a living by the pen. Professional writers are expected to be accurate. So research is more than nice; it's mandatory and it must be done with care.

CHAPTER FIVE

Sidebars and Photos

Sidebars and photos aren't the meat and potatoes of selling, but tasty side dishes that enhance the overall flavor of the meal and increase its value.

They do deserve special attention, though, particularly if you want to earn a healthy income from writing. You must know how they fit into the larger scheme of selling, when they can make the difference to a sale, and how and when they can or should be offered or provided.

When should you use sidebars?

Sometimes you need more than a simple, self-contained article to make the sale or to explain the topic fully. Sidebars accompany perhaps a third of the magazine articles sold, so you must know what they are and how they enhance your salability to editors. The good news: They usually earn you more money!

You may hear sidebars referred to as bars or boxes. They're the same thing: secondary information linked to an article and contained in a box or sidebar.

Time and *Newsweek* use them all the time, often shaded a different color to set them off. If the main story is about welfare change, the box will probably contain an in-depth account of how the changes affect one welfare family. Or a list of the changes in the law.

If you're writing about the turnip festival in Tulip, Michigan, your box might be (1) other town activities this year, (2) other points of interest to see within forty miles of Tulip, (3) a thumbnail history of the town and township, (4) six national figures born in Tulip.

You get the idea: If the main article covers the broad theme (taxation, life on Mars, illegal immigrants), the sidebar zeroes in (a state that lowers taxes annually, how microbes can exist in hostile environments, one family living in three countries). Macro/micro.

Or the reverse: The article is about type B blood and the difficulty of matching donors in Finland, Spain and Bolivia; the box tells how the mutant blood type began and spread. Or the article is a biography of Sandy Koufax; the box tells of Jewish ballplayers in the major leagues. Micro/macro.

Which editors use sidebars?

Most do, but you must study the publication to see if the one you want to buy your masterpiece is in the majority. Newspaper editors are the most likely buyers, particularly if the box is short and tucks up in an empty hole near the article.

They create more problems for magazine editors, who are crimped for space. So they are more likely to break the article into components, the body and a box or two (before or after) only if they know in advance the total space needed and why the sidebar adds appreciably to the article's content.

How do you sell sidebars?

For newspapers or to other simultaneous submission editors, since you don't query, you really only have two means to get the additional copy accepted and bought.

The best is probably just to write the box at the same time you write the article, create and print up each manuscript separately, and on the top of the sidebar, write in large letters "SIDEBAR" so the editor knows it is supplementary material. Then the editor has four choices: (1) buy the article alone, (2) buy the article and the sidebar, (3) buy only the sidebar or (4) send you packing, sans sale whatever.

It's a rare day they do the third, although not so rare for them to kindly refuse the article for some reason but ask you to expand the sidebar into another article with a new slant they suggest.

Rest assured, option two will never happen if you don't send in a good sidebar that adds significantly to the original piece. Three would never happen without a sidebar to see, and sometimes an article is so full of minutiae and detail, ideal for sidebars, that if all left in one article it is unbuyable. Those are the positives, beyond the fact that a sidebar increases your income, sometimes doubling it.

The negative is the loss of time writing sidebars that are unbought.

An example might help clarify the process.

Some years back I became interested in gray whales and their near extinction in California, where I had recently moved. In researching the topic, I discovered that one could take a three-hour boat trip from the San Pedro harbor, near Los Angeles, to see the giant critters up close, or as close as they want you to be.

I bobbed and exclaimed in awe with the other fair-weather gawkers as the whales appeared, blew mist, breathed and gracefully disappeared. After interviewing the captain and first mate, I found my land legs and spoke to the founder of the Whale Watch program at the nearby Maritime Museum, which also had an excellent exhibit about the oldest and largest extant mammals. The result was an article about how one could see gray whales by ship off the southern California coast.

My choice was to cram another thousand words of details into that magic prose about precisely which cities had wharves housing ships that took the public on such excursions, where the wharves were, the names of the ships, their whale-watching schedules, the costs, phone numbers for amplification and other particulars—or set those aside in a box and let the editors decide if the box, all or part, was wanted for their pages.

As it turned out, six editors bought the article and all paid extra and bought the sidebar too. More often, a few buy it all but most have room only for the main offering.

I mentioned two ways to sell sidebars to newspapers or simultaneous submission markets. The second is to suggest, in the cover note accompanying the finished manuscript, that you could write a sidebar, then explain what it would say and why it would add significantly to the article. (Savvy editors would ask themselves why, if it's so valuable, you didn't just write and send it.)

I dislike the second process for two reasons. One, there is too little room as it is in the cover note, and what there is should be used to sell the article itself and to explain the availability of photos. Two, the editors must put the article aside, contact you about the sidebar, wait until it arrives and then pump up their enthusiasm a second time about the article, if they can still find it. The newspaper world spins too quickly for that many variables; too many sales will be lost. Better to take the chance, write a sidebar if it's needed and get something bought at the first reading.

For magazines, time loss writing unbought boxes is far less likely. You will mention the possibility of a sidebar in your query letter first, and only if the editor encourages its creation and submission will you invest the extra effort needed.

That will also better guide you when you prepare the article itself. With a sidebar you can focus on one aspect of the topic and leave the other details, or the critical points uncovered, to the bar. Without it, you must touch every base in the text.

Another cetaceous example, a bit convoluted, shows what I mean.

I had just sent a finished manuscript to *Dynamic Years* about "Whale Watching in the United States" when, in an airplane seated next to me, I met a sea captain who had been contracted to capture the only gray whale in existence, Gigi, kept in San Diego's Sea World. Since he too was captive, I interviewed Frank Mason and asked if he minded if I shared his adventure with the world.

The next morning I called the editor of *Dynamic Years*, explained my good fortune and suggested that the core of the interview might make an interesting sidebar. He agreed. I wrote it up that afternoon, mailed it (during the era when a fax was presumably a female fox), and the article and sidebar, in size, suddenly became the lead piece and required a cover photo to match!

The order was backward—95 percent of the sidebars I've sold to magazines were suggested in the query letter and developed as a result of the editor's interest—but the end result was the same: a better writing product, more complete with more facts, quotes and anecdotes. A subject better developed, balanced between two angles. And a fatter paycheck for not a whole lot more work.

A last point: How and where do you suggest a sidebar in a query letter?

If at all, I like to do it dead last, after I've sold the idea. My last paragraph might read: "If interested, I can also provide a sidebar about Frank Mason, the only sea captain who ever captured a gray whale (Gigi, for San Diego's Sea World). Since you require those interviewed to be 45+, Frank, at 63, is fair game. Just let me know."

If you have two possible sidebars, the same format: "I can also provide sidebars about (A), with a quick explanation, and/or (B), with an explanation, if interested. Just let me know." Three is too many. One, if too long, is too many. Keep the focus in a query on the primary topic, and only suggest a sidebar if it's an interesting, valuable addition that adds a second dimension.

How much are sidebars worth?

Certainly less than the article itself. Sometimes the editor won't pay a penny extra, thinking that the text is all part of a larger article, however divided. But that's rare.

Newspapers might pay you from $25 to $100 more. Magazines often increase the pay from 10 to 50 percent depending on the amount of work or research required. The truth is, you are left to the mercy or charity of the editor.

Often the real payment becomes obvious later. A well-structured article that includes a sidebar, even two, convinces the editor you are the kind of professional who should write often for her pages—main pieces, usually on assignment, travel paid. The payment is delayed but considerably more over the long run than the few extra bucks earned now for going the extra mile.

Can sidebars be sold any other way?

Sell your words any way you can. You can break an epic into one hundred short poems and sell each to a different editor, if you wish. Sidebars can be sold as add-ons to an article, then rewritten and sold as a short article or a filler to another magazine. If you can find forty different ways the same facts can be resorted into clearly distinct items, you have forty different products to sell.

But note the word *rewrite*. You get hopelessly enmeshed in the rights issue unless you change the title, the lead, the conclusion and the order—that is, decidedly reslant each version. Once reslanted, go to it. You may even need a sidebar to your reformulated sidebar. If so, follow the process above!

When should you provide photos?

If you have usable photos of your own or at your disposal, offer them for review and possible purchase.

Travel photography is by far the most frequently bought, though historical and sports photos are often sought as well. But any photos might be purchased if they add to the overall quality of the final presentation.

Assuming you've already taken the trip or been to the focal spot of the travel piece and have photos of the quality used by the publication, mention that in the query or cover letter, as we saw in earlier chapters.

If a particular photo is extraordinary—a salamander devouring a tourist or the shopping mall on the lost Island of Atlantis—by all means elaborate upon that in full. Offering twenty-four or thirty-six top-quality slides or black-and-white prints about the locale for the editor's perusal is more common, hoping that in your assortment of photographic baubles the editor will find some priceless jewels.

As likely, you have yet to take the trip and are querying in advance. In that case, indicate that you are a competent photographer ("214 travel photos sold," "I photograph all shots used in my column," etc.) and ask if the editor wants you to submit photos with your copy when you return. If so, any particular photo preference—or advice? If the editor nods yes, study the last three issues of that publication to see what that editor (with the art editor) buys.

Are the photos in color or black and white? Are they vertical or horizontal? Do they feature people? Doing what? How are they dressed? How directly related are the photos to the key points of the article, or are they supplementary sites to broaden its coverage? Are there captions?

That tells you how and where to point the camera, the kind of film to use and whether you need additional facts for the captions.

Color or black and white?

While you can convert color slides into black-and-white prints, the process is a bit costly and there is some loss of sharpness. So taking both normally requires the use of two cameras, each 35mm or larger.

You will usually know by studying earlier issues of the target publications whether they use one format or both. But if you simply don't know or you find a new topic to explore while on a trip, presume that magazines almost always use color slides (with an occasional black and white on the inside pages) and newspapers usually buy black and white from freelancers (saving the color for the main article, usually written by the travel editor or an associate).

Rough guidelines for color slides

As this book is being written, photography is in the midst of a technological revolution, with digital photos being instantly scannable on computers and sent by modem (or satellite) across the world. So much of what I say sounds antiquated and inferior because it is tied to the technology of yesteryear. Yet magazines change slowly and editors will continue to accept and use good photos however they arrive, so at some peril I will continue to explain how it has been done for the past thirty years and let you adjust the desired results to the evolving means.

The purpose is to provide sharp, revealing color slides about the topic. That means studying the publication, then supplying photos of every aspect of the article possible. I used as a guide two rolls of 36-exposure film as a backdrop if I didn't have a go-ahead. That immediately shot up to six to eight rolls if I got the nod.

Try to get the full color spectrum in as many shots as possible. Nature gives you plenty of blues, browns, greens and grays. You need reds and yellows to complete the rainbow. To do that you can stand your subjects in a blooming poppy patch. You can find the reds and yellows from the surrounding features. Or if all else fails, you can dress your subject, or models you plant near them in the crowd, in red and yellow. (My daughters spent much of their vacation youth dressed in reds and yellows when we visited writing locales!)

Build your photo components of each article around one (or several) photo "grabbers," shots that instantly tell what the story is about: a fourteen-year-old Colorado Indian in central Ecuador, his stout body evenly painted with bright red clay, yellow feathers poking through his matted hair, with a yellow loincloth his attire, a hot dog in one hand and a cola in the other. The photo sets the story: Ecuador, Indians, tradition, change.

The crumbling shell of a rural Nebraska farm, eighty years collapsing, with a tree growing through the porch roof. A gravestone in front reads

> **Thomas Crowley**
> Born 1891
> **Louise Crowley**
> Born 1894
> **Four children**
> All died in 1916
> from smallpox

Take many photos of the "grabbers" to convey the message as many ways as you can, bracketing your f-stops, shooting at different hours (sunrise, noon, sunset), changing backdrops to vary your firing focus. Then complete the background by gathering a wide assortment of related views from varying angles: wide angle, zoom, close-up, horizon.

Unless they are crowd shots, get the names of as many people in the photos as possible. Even better, their addresses, ages, occupations and anything more directly linked to the topic. Keep this in a notepad. Jot down the slide numbers so you can more easily correlate the data when the developed slides return.

If you focus on one person, particularly with close-up shots, you need his name and address should you later need to secure photo releases.

How often are photo releases required? Rarely. *Writer's Market* tells which publications routinely require them. In those cases, when you query, ask the editor, if interested in the article, would she please also send you a photo release and all necessary instructions?

Otherwise, if needed and you have kept the names, you can get the necessary signatures later.

A tip: When you photoshoot people or near-people, if at all possible, catch them doing something germane to the topic (a fisherman tying a mosquito fly, a scrub lady sound asleep on the subway with a bear grip on her frayed purse, a fly on a cross-eyed bear's nose).

After the slides are taken, have them developed and put in paper mounts. Then adhere a stick-on name tag to each slide you send to the editor for review. Insert the slides in a plastic slide-holder (available at any photo shop, four rows high and five across) and write a caption sheet for each holder. Indicate by row and number (Row 2, Slide 3) what each slide shows, in a sentence or two. Attach the caption sheet to the holder with staples so you can lift it up and see the slides below. Add your name and address to each caption sheet. Send the slide-holders with the magazine article, with a large manila envelope, addressed and stamped, to get the slides back.

The editor will keep the preferred slides, often four to eight, returning the rest. The kept slides will usually be returned after the article has been printed, with one or several copies of that issue of the magazine.

Do you send all of your slides? Your response is based on the value of the shots. If you have plenty of salable slides and they aren't once-in-a-century valuable, send originals.

But if the slides are particularly valuable, have copies made of the best and send those copies in a different plastic holder for the editor's selection, explaining that the duplicates should be returned with an indication of those preferred so the originals can subsequently be sent, by registered mail. The editor indicates those wanted, returning all of the duplicates. Then send the originals of the chosen few, also a plastic holder, heavily insured. The system is cumbersome but it works. I've used it for years and never lost a slide or a client.

Rough guidelines for black-and-white photos

Almost all of the black and whites you sell will be to newspapers, so there are a few things one must remember when serving that medium by camera.

One, newspapers buy far more vertical photos than horizontal, since it is a vertical format and they better fit the column structure. So see and shoot vertically, given a choice. A dachshund, an eminently horizontal animal, is vertical face-on. A tree or a building against the horizon becomes a vertical view.

Two, newspaper printing leaves the details and contrasts indistinct,

---

Will Editors Buy Magazine Cover Photos From Freelancers?

Sure. If your slides are so compelling that they shout to be used on the cover, editors will hear the noise. But don't count on it happening often. There are professional photographers with far better batting averages in that league to whom the editors customarily turn for front cover mastery.

Three things are imperative to even get up to bat: It must be in color, the slide must be a vertical (how many covers are black and white or horizontal?) and it must be sharp.

So if you see something through the lens that has cover potential, grab the camera with color film, shoot it vertically and bracket it (if you're manually setting f-stops.)

When you submit your slides, gently suggest that the editor might consider slide *x* or slides *a* and *b* as possible cover shots. That's it. If chosen, it usually means a windfall of $300–$1,000. If not, you have some super shots to be used with the text.

---

so early morning or late afternoon shots often loose their sharpness. Dark complexions in dark clothes against dark settings do the same. Sharp black-and-white definition works best.

Three, newspapers customarily use captions with the shots, so you must dredge up more detail to explain what the camera has caught: locations and names, correctly spelled, with proper titles, if appropriate. Also, the names of specific events and the time of day (or season).

Four, catch people doing what the photo should show. A hang glider pilot should be adjusting gear, running to launch, hang gliding or landing. Dressed in civvies drinking a beer and sharing lies doesn't cut it: How do you know photographically that the person isn't a fisherman or fighter pilot?

My quota when covering topics that lent themselves to newspaper purchase—which usually meant travel or fast-breaking news in remote places where I happened to be—was a minimum of three black-and-white rolls 36-exposure, more if it was hot news.

Photo releases are of less concern to newspapers as long as they are taken in or from public places—that means any place not clearly marked or understood to be private. Parks, streets, sidewalks, markets are fine. Some "public" places *aren't* to cameras, however, so always check the photo policies at museums, zoos and theaters.

Newspapers ultimately want 8×10s to reduce to the needed insert size, but they pay too little ($10–$50 per photo used) for you to afford to send them those initial enlargements. And you don't know which of the shots they want enlarged anyway.

So let me suggest a submission system that has worked smoothly for me for thirty years, as a base for improvements while photographic technology takes hold.

I send my rolls to a developer, requesting proof (or contact) sheets, not prints. I receive a sheet of contact paper, about $9'' \times 12''$, on which my 35mm negative strips have been laid, and the photos have been developed the same size as the negative itself. A thin plastic envelope containing the negative strips accompanies the proof sheets.

In the meantime, as we saw earlier, I've sent a cover note attached to the article simultaneously submitted to many newspaper travel editors in which I asked if the editors would be interested in receiving sixteen proofs to select from, or the five best. While I await their responses, I attach the negatives in an envelope to the back of the respective proof sheets and store them in a file.

When an editor asks for the sixteen for selection, I take out the three proof sheets (one per roll of film), detach the negatives from the back and select the best sixteen shots that match that article's theme. Since they are for newspaper use, I pick two-thirds to three-fourths of the total from the verticals.

I then cut out the chosen photos from the proof sheets, arrange them in some sensible order, adhere them four rows across and four rows down on a regular sheet of $8\frac{1}{2}'' \times 11''$ paper (using double-stick tape or Scotch tape) and add row/shot numbers so the accompanying caption sheet, explaining what each photo is about, is easy to match. Both look like the example on the following page.

On both the sixteen-proof sheet and the caption sheet, I add the article subject and my name and address. (I also copy the caption sheet. Editors never return it but often have questions about one or

Proof Sheet   Caption Sheet

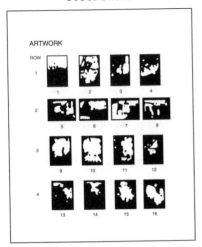

several items on it.)

To the newspaper travel editor requesting my photography, I send the sixteen-proof sheet, the caption sheet and a short note as shown in the example on page 81.

The editor sends back the sixteen-proof sheet, sometimes circling the negatives requested or including a note indicating those wanted. Often that is done on the back of the short note I sent. I then carefully cut those negatives from the strips, insert them into small plastic negative sleeves (or envelopes, available at photo supply stores), copy the request from the editor and add a note to it requesting the return of the negatives as soon as they are duplicated (with thanks).

Soon enough a copy or two of the article arrive, accompanied by the negatives and a check. Or they arrive separately. But they always arrive: Neither the negatives nor the check has ever failed to arrive. Sometimes you have to ask for a copy of the article!

If the editor requests your five best, the process is much the same: Three of the five will be vertical, and you can include both the proof photos and the captions on the same page. You also send the negatives at the same time.

Should you take both color and black-and-white photos?

You bet, unless you know that you need only one format for one article.

Usually you will be traveling, with some go-aheads at hand, some

(Your Name)
(Your Address)
(City, State ZIP)
(Date)

Dear _____ (Editor's Name):

I've chosen the best 16 from my proof sheets, 12 vertical and 4 horizontal. Please let me know which negatives to send and if you need more information for those shots than appears on the enclosed caption sheet. Would you please return this proof sheet with your reply, in the SASE? Thanks.

(Your Signature)

solid ideas you want to pursue on site and newspaper pieces to compose later. So you have only a rough idea of what you absolutely need (the go-ahead photos) but no idea of the photos that will best match after-the-trip magazine or newspaper pieces.

The dumbest thing you can do, other than failing to get the facts, quotes and anecdotes that supply the heart of the article you are illustrating, is to take too few photos. Better to take an extra roll or two or five, slides and black and white, than to have to return to Oslo or Oman to get more photos.

Mailing your photos

To mail photos, pack the large sixteen black-and-white print pages inside cardboard inserts and write on the envelope in large letters "PHOTOS—DO NOT BEND." Put the photos in a protective plastic bag (freezer or even sandwich bags are fine), and include your manuscript in the same envelope. Also, send it first-class or priority mail.

Slides are less risky to mail because of the sturdy acetate holders with twenty slots into which one slide each can be inserted. Put these sheets between cardboard inserts to prevent damage. Do not use glass mounts!

Part Two

STRATEGIES
FOR SELLING

CHAPTER SIX

Magazine Selling by Query Letter

N othing is as important to magazine editors as the query letter. It is the first thing they see from a publishing hopeful, and if not done well and properly, the last.

Before researching and writing a magazine article, you first research and write a one-page query letter. It asks, in essence, whether that editor would even consider using your idea, slant, special word order and form-fitting of the topic to her readers before you invest your valuable time and skills.

Let's take an in-depth look at what query letters are, what makes them almost legal tender when done right and what they look like.

What is a query and what should it say?

In the simplest of terms, a query letter is a question, an inquiry, to an editor. The question is, "Would you be interested in (the subject of your article)?" Since editors of publications that appear in print need to both consider the idea and see whether its proponent can write sufficiently well to adapt that idea to their pages, that question becomes the core of a letter that expounds upon the idea written in the style of the article its author proposes to submit.

Not all queries are made by letter. Later in this chapter, we'll discuss when querying might be better done by fax, by e-mail, by phone or in person. Devote such creativity to the manuscript only after it is sold—

successfully selling the conventional way, by letter sent snail mail, is hard enough.

Certain components must appear in every query: the topic you want the editor to consider, your name and how you can be contacted. Also commonly included is some mention of your published credits, your special preparation or expertise in dealing with the topic, the key sources that will be used, perhaps the names of those to be interviewed, the type and quality of illustrations to be submitted with the manu-script (if any) and enough factual material about the topic to convince the editor that readers would benefit from and enjoy reading your article.

Yet query letters differ, and not every query needs all of the elements mentioned—and some need even more. It all gets back to the purpose of the query, which dictates what you must include, and sometimes in what order.

As we discussed in chapters one and two, the purpose of queries is straightforward. You want to sell your writing—and editors must buy good writing to fill their pages. The query letter serves as a visual bridge that lets you display your idea in words that convince the editor that the promised copy—the article that develops the idea in full form—is precisely what is needed for a coming issue!

Query letters are time-savers that let you test an idea before having to complete the research, conduct interviews, take photos and write the manuscript. Instead, you conduct a feasibility study, lightly researching your idea to see if a full article can be written about it and if what you promise in the letter can indeed result in the promised article. When you are certain your article is worth writing and can be written, you write a query letter asking if the editor would be interested in using such an idea/article in his publication.

The letter adds another, critical dimension, whether stated or im-plied. It is that your article will be specifically written for that editor's readers. It will be molded around their desires, interests, gender, age, reading level, quirks. In other words, not so many words off the shelf written to whomever it may concern, but rather text created explicitly for the subscribers and buyers of that editor's publication.

The editor presumes that as a professional you haven't already writ-ten the article without knowing in advance that it would be seriously considered for his pages. That you wouldn't waste your time and energy so recklessly. And that if you speak of your article as a reality in the query, it is a sort of virtual reality that will be created when the affirmative reply is received.

You are your query letter

Remember, all the editor knows about you is what can be read on one page of paper, in your letter. If the letter is written on spotted butcher paper, what does that say about you? If it contains three missplelled (*sic*) words in the first paragraph, does it show a solid command of written English? If the query is dull yet promises an exciting article, which should be believed, the promise or the evidence? Editors are as human as we are, and they like others to succeed, especially when that success adds to their own. Gain their confidence with solid query letters, then make good on the gain with copy as good or better than that promised. That's a formula certain to tame and win any editor.

Let's look at a magazine query letter, then examine why it was written as it was. The example begins on the next page.

The components of a successful query letter

Now let's take a detailed look at the elements that every successful query letter must have.

Subject

Again, the purpose of your query letter is to sell an idea, then a manuscript about that idea for publication. The heart of your query letter is that idea. Everything else is secondary. The tone of the proposed topic will likewise dictate the tone of your letter, the way you talk about and develop your idea. If the subject is serious—child abuse, bankruptcy, caring for the gravely ill—the tone of the query must also be serious. If the topic is fluffy and fun, the letter should show evidence of that same light joy. Which is not to say that it should be silly and pointless, rather that it must enhance the manuscript's consideration, and sale, by showing your ability to write the piece as you wrote the query. If you propose to write a funny article but the query letter is flatter than Iowa, utterly alien to humor, what would the editor's first suspicion be? You'd like to write funny stuff but clearly can't.

Gordon Burgett
(Address)
(City, State ZIP)
(Phone/Fax)
(Date)

Editor's Name
Managing Editor, Magazine
Street Address
City, State ZIP

Dear _____ (Editor's Name):

The word *Alzheimer* gets all readers' attention. If not an aunt or grandfather, is the disease patiently awaiting them? When will it strike? Was the forgotten telephone number or calling one's daughter by the cat's name the first sign?

I'd like to go a step wider and create a state-of-the-art piece for _____ readers about dementia, the "reduced intellectual and emotional abilities that interfere with independent functioning." Dementia includes Alzheimer's disease, which comprises about 70 percent of the cases, affecting some four million older Americans now and predicted to rise to fourteen million in 2050. Most of the rest suffer from vascular (blood vessel) diseases, which can also be a secondary cause of Alzheimer's.

The article would define dementia (by example as well as words), then explain the risk factors, current research findings, treatment and home care. It would describe in detail the kind of comprehensive workup required at the outset of the first symptoms; what we know now about the causes of dementia (including genetic chromosomal mutations, high blood pressure, immune system toxicity); possible means of prevention, postponement or treatment (aspirin, other nonsteroidal anti-inflammatories, estrogen replacement therapy, tactrine), and more accurate ways of detecting dementia in all forms (including chromosome testing, PET and MRI scans, neurological testing, even the possibility that it can be seen in writing samples of a young adult in the writing's idea density and grammatical complexity).

Rather than a cold, clinical recitation of facts, the article would be built around the questions anybody would have about dementia, answered through facts and quotes (from leading researchers, caregivers and families of sufferers), plus anecdotes interwoven. If you're interested, I could also include a sidebar that looks at the future of dementia detection and treatment.

While I have had 1,600+ articles in print (plus fifteen books) about a wide range of topics, I've concentrated the past two years on dentistry and the primary care medical field. Am I demented in thinking that your readers are eager to know of the increasing rays of hope in this field, how the newest discoveries apply to their families and themselves and if testing now is possible or even advisable?

Respectfully,

Gordon Burgett

Too often query letters fail to show the writer's grasp of the subject. They are too short and the facts too few for the editor to conclude more than that the writer has mailed out several hundred once-over-quickly suggestions and will later research those topics about which any editor shows interest.

One way to assure there is enough depth is to think of the query letter as a précis or single-page summary of a piece already written, from which you selected the best elements that explain the subject and how you will present it. Such summary queries might include the subject and your approach to it, supporting data, the conclusions to be drawn and the reason why a reader should even care about the topic in the first place, if that isn't obvious.

Expertise or preparation

Editors will want to know how you got or will get your facts, if they are reliable and accurate and how well you know the field.

This is particularly important when writing for specialized journals. Editors in the medical field, for example, aren't waiting for a vague piece from a layperson who thinks canker sores might be cured someday. On the other hand, they would indeed be interested in cures, methods of treatment or scientific studies on the causes and treatments of similar viral afflictions in the U.S. and elsewhere. You needn't be a doctor or a scientist to write for their pages, but you must have a firm understanding of the subject, accurate and accessible sources and probably verifiable quotes from experts—all explained in your query so the editor has only to give you a go-ahead and wait for reliable, accurate copy for the publication.

So in the query you tell the editor what you can provide and from what source.

Should you mention your academic background in the query? Only if (1) that background gives you special insight into the topic, (2) it provides you with a unique understanding of the topic, (3) you are writing about academia or (4) you are writing to academics. The editors would probably be as or more impressed if you had written for other journals similar to theirs about a like topic.

Two editor friends laughed when I asked how they would respond to a list of earned degrees in a query letter. Their replies were the same: "That's fine, but can the person write? And can the reader believe what the person says?"

Previous publications

If you have never been in print before, say nothing.

If you have a few clips and they fall into the church bulletin and hometown newspaper category, silence is again the best policy—unless your writing is extensive in either and you're branching out from that base. Mention previous publications only if they are impressive. If the query letter itself shouts "professional," their absence won't summarily eliminate you. If the query letter proves you are a beginner, one hundred publications in alphabetical order won't make much difference. They won't be believed.

If you've sold to that publication before, mention it, particularly if another editor reigned during the earlier sale. If you wish to show an editor you've worked a wide range of fields when you're proposing a subject with particularly broad appeal, give a more extensive list. If the field is narrow, niched or highly specialized, focus on those publications that discuss the same general topic, with perhaps a few other, impressive publications added in.

There's a temptation for beginners to puff their credits—to raise a real three to a fictitious thirty-three—by citing magazines they wish they had sold to. A foolish game, really. You will be judged on the manuscript prepared in response to a query go-ahead, and if it shows too little writing skill, not only will the piece be rejected, the editor will wonder how you could have sold so often before. Your name will stick, negatively, and it may well be harder for you to break into print with that editor the next time around. Even worse, what if the editor asks to see specific examples of your previous work?

Sometimes a market write-up does request tearsheets, clips or samples of earlier published work. An editor occasionally makes the same request after reading a query. I have a contrary bias here. When newcomers send clips with their queries, the editor first reads the query, then the clips. Too often the clips are so unlike what the writer is promising in the query (the previous articles were somber and the letter promises humor, or they were light and general and the editor needs facts, quotes and details deftly interwoven) that the editor isn't convinced the writer can provide what he says. At the least the editor doubts the writer's wisdom in sending copies so unlike what he is proposing. So the editor rejects the query. I think it's because the writer showed too much.

My conclusion: Don't send clips unless specifically asked by the editor in response to your query, if you are asked at all. That is, despite what the editor requests in the current write-up in *Writer's Market*, at most indicate that clips will gladly be sent—but don't send them with the query. (Many of my editor friends disagree with me, so feel free to include them when querying. On the other hand, my bias worked well enough to get me 1,600 sales.)

At least, don't send in a friend's article or something you wish you had written and say it is yours, written under a pseudonym! If this is your first submission or you've yet to make a sale and thus have no examples to send and the editor asks for your clips, just tell her that her publication will soon be in the envious position of publishing your very first magazine article—and that article will be the clipping you show the world of future editors! Lucky her, número uno!

But if the editor requests clips in response to your query and you have them, try to find examples as close to the editor's publication as you can, without too much regard to date, although you might include a copy of your most recent piece too if the other examples are from Ike's era. If you have very few sales but examples are asked for, send photocopies of what you do have.

Illustrations

These are usually photographs but can also include slides, drawings, maps, charts and other items used to illustrate your manuscript.

As we saw in chapter five, travel pieces very often require photographs. But there are other types of articles that also require illustrations. If you are trying to sell a bloodracer called "How I Caught a 400-Pound Pirarucu," you had better have more than one dim slide showing you in an Amazonian setting with a garlike, tongued fish larger than yourself. Likewise, a story about hiking the lost trail across the Andean *páramo* had better come with slides or photos of a trail devoid of Baby Ruth candy-bar wrappers in a setting convincingly Ecuadorian.

The number of photos and slides you can provide will interest the editor, as will their size and quality. Unless it is germane to the story, who took them is less important than that they were taken. It's not uncommon for a writer to be working out of his home while trustworthy photographer friends or hired professionals are snapping shots for him halfway across the country. Or to have a graphics colleague or professional create comical drawings to illustrate humor pieces, enlarging markets for both of them.

Should you send illustrations with the query letter? No, mostly because they can get lost en route or go astray at the destination. Mention what you can provide in the query, then wait until the editor requests samples.

Why this query is written as it is

Subject. A huge concern right now is Alzheimer's, and I too am interested because of the havoc it is bringing to friends and co-workers who have parents so afflicted. Yet I've been confused about whether the old term "dementia" is the same thing as Alzheimer's. If I'm confused, so are others—that's where I find my best ideas. A few hours of probing not only cleared that up, it suggested that what most are sweeping under the Alzheimer's rug may indeed be something else, perhaps curable, maybe even preventable, and certainly should be universally understood. This will be a straightforward piece, short on humor, long on making technical terms and foot-long protein names understandable. The query is written in the same form. (Always write the query like the copy to follow.)

Expertise or preparation. Just put in the numbers and that I've dwelt heavily on medicine and dentistry lately and let that imply that I too could write about Alzheimer's.

Previous publications. Not much room in this query. And I've not written about this topic before so I keep it broad enough, telling where I will go for information. If the editor wants more, she will ask.

Illustrations. I have none in mind, so I don't mention illustrations.

Other. I selected this query because it has so few particulars the form would work for almost any topic, except those involving humor. A page full of what I'd like to write about that also explains why the reader would be interested.

What a query letter shouldn't say

A query letter should be positive. Tell the editor the idea you wish to develop, what tools and special skills you bring to the task, information about your past writing experience and so on. The rest remains unsaid. It's hard enough to sell an idea in a good query letter without saying too much and creating doubt.

Thus a letter asking for editorial or writer's guidelines, while a good idea before querying, is not a query. Nor is a letter asking an editor what is needed, a letter to avoid because it shows ou have no concept of what a writer should do: Provide both ideas and manuscripts.

Previous publications

For example, you should not mention that you've never, or seldom, been in print before. You should not attempt to overwhelm the editor with your honesty and frankness, hoping to woo that lucky soul into giving you your first big break by laying your record bare. Nor should you lie and invent publications or an impressive number of items supposedly sold—or claim that you used to write under the name of Jack London or Louisa May Alcott. Don't say a word. Rather, let a tight, fast, professional-sounding query letter tell the real truth, at least by implication: This idea is from a writer able and eager to produce good copy needed by the publication (whether or not that writer has sold before). Write so well that the editor is thinking about how to get you to write for the magazine again and again.

The writer's gender

If you're a woman and want to write for a male magazine, or the reverse, a man for the ladies' pages, just go to it, but consider using only your initials instead of your name. Appear as B.R. Hawkins in a hockey story for *Boys Will Be Boys*, rather than as Bobbie Rae. Unless the sex switch is important to the piece—"I Was the First Female Boxer in Latvia"—I'd write the query, give initials or a name in keeping with the topic, produce first-class copy and cash the check.

Money

Newcomers are best advised to keep questions about cash out of the query.

Writer's Market lists payment rates, so you should have an idea at the outset about the amount you can expect. (The amount paid for first-time purchases generally sticks close to the listed rates; a modest increase can be expected in later purchases.) It's also common for an editor in a query response to indicate a proposed pay rate, plus information about article length, deadline and sometimes slant. If you have absolutely no idea what an editor might pay, you can write the publication before querying and ask to receive a "guideline for writers sheet" and, if it's not included, any information about customary pay range.

Once you know the rough pay range, if you can't produce your copy and profit within that frame, it makes sense to seek out another topic or publication where that can be done.

There are too many unknowns about a new writer for an editor to even consider upping the ante on a first article. A request for higher payment before the copy is seen will usually get both the request and the article quickly rejected.

Save that for later, if necessary—preferably your third or fourth sale to the same editor. But if you simply must ask the first or second time out, at least wait until the editor responds with a query go-ahead and has shown some interest in the topic and you.

Later on, after you've been writing for a while, you will gain a feel for this kind of thing and will know your steady buyers and their ways, as well as their actual pay ranges. Then, if the money made simply doesn't cover costs or a fair profit, you have two choices: Adjust the costs or haggle, lovingly, to get the publication to help with or totally pay your expenses.

Alas, most magazines won't pay travel for new writers, and many won't pay expenses on any kind of speculation (not assigned) go-aheads.

Lack of knowledge of the subject

If you have an uplifting desire to write a piece about ballooning and sail off a query on the subject, don't confide in the editor that "you know nothing about ballooning but will learn through research"—or would love to take your first ride if the publication will just pay your way!

If the editor is lukewarm about the subject anyway, that interest will quickly float off. Or if the subject does strike the editor's fancy, you'll be passed over for somebody better informed. Your obligation is to learn about the topic *before* querying so that the slant suggested and the support material mentioned will be accurate, and the article proposed can be written. Then if you get a go-ahead and you learn about ballooning while completing your research, that is your business. The editor's interest is in a solid, reliable article about ballooning, not how and when your knowledge was gained.

Writers needn't be experts on every subject they cover. Yet to query with no knowledge and to expect an editor to pay you to learn the basic facts is to underestimate the seriousness of professional writing.

Pseudonyms

Editors get very nervous when you use a pseudonym, assuming immediately that you have sprinkled libelous heresy throughout your prose and left them to carry the litigious bag. "The author? Sorry, we have no idea who he/she is—that's just the name they wrote under. Of course we'll pay the suit."

If it's for affectation, forget it. If you're the deacon of your church and grinding out scurrilous pornography, change your name. For the rest, you'd better have a solid reason and be willing to file a fictitious business statement so you can cash the check. Or figure out another way to get the editor to pay you, and keep your moniker secret or silent.

To which editor should you write?

The best way to find out to whom the query letter should be sent is to check the current *Writer's Market*. If it says "send all queries to Ms. Elsie Martin, Managing Editor," the only remaining question is whether she still holds the same position. Check the most recent issue of the publication, then send your query to Martin or the current managing editor.

If the *Writer's Market* listing doesn't indicate a person or position, try the managing editor or the section editor where your idea would most likely appear. The larger the publication, the less likely you should be writing directly to the editor in chief, or equivalent. More often, the managing editor or section editor weeds through queries, pulls the most promising, works them into idea possibilities for coming issues and takes those workups to the editor in chief for discussion and/or approval, replying to you after a decision has been made.

What a Good Query Looks Like

A query letter is a business letter, not a chatty, informal "how's-the-family" exchange between old friends, even if the editor, by chance, also happens to be family or an old friend. You are asking for money in exchange for a service. You want to be paid for researching, writing and permitting the use of your labors.

So the appropriate form for such a transaction is that of a business letter: concise, direct and functional. The examples in this book show one form of business letter. For variations, consult your library for books describing and showing other forms.

Query letters should be single-spaced. Well crafted, you should be able to fit everything needed on one page. They should be neat, error-free and written on white paper, unless one consistently uses a very light gray, cream or pastel. Flaming red, white and blue queries or undue computer legerdemain, like white type on reversed, black paper, shout "showboat" and create doubt in the editor's mind about your seriousness, maturity or perhaps even sanity.

Put in another light, if you ran an ad asking for all qualified writers interested in preparing your biography to appear at a certain address at a stated time and three showed up, without knowing more than you could see (as is true for an editor with a query letter in hand), would you most likely hire (1) a person neat in appearance, clean and dressed in conventional form, (2) a person with a dash of mud artlessly scattered about his face and clothing, with a tear in one shoe and a price tag hanging from one sleeve, or (3) a person wearing a three-foot-tall hat with pigeon feathers poking from it, a blazing violet neck wrap that partially obscured her face and most of her torso and electric yellow-blue high-heeled work boots?

A conventional business letter is analogous to (1). In form, not too exciting, but not too alarming either. No distractions delay or obstruct consideration of the writer's message. The second person might be like an error-filled, slapdash letter. If its writer thinks so little of the letter's appearance, can he be trusted to do a thorough job researching an article? Will the final manuscript show adherence to accuracy? Maybe, but the editor has to overcome serious misgivings created by the letter's first impression.

A third letter might bring to mind the third person: a screaming missive on scarlet paper printed in green, smelling of perfume (or is it rum?) and spiced with such starred and underlined "grabbers" as "Reply Instantly," "Chance-of-a-Lifetime," "I'm Your Person," etc. It shouts so many hair-raising messages that an editor, whose reputation and scalp depend upon the writer's output, couldn't help but have grave doubts.

The point is simple: Let the body of the letter sell both your idea and you as the person who should prepare it. The form of the letter should be so secondary, and supportive, that nothing delays the reader from leaping into the written message. Neither errors nor strikeovers, hand-scribbled footnotes, eye-yanking arrows, gaudy paper or a parade of 24-point Wingdings should pull the reader's attention from the letter's crucial contents. Everything in the letter, stated and implied, should work in your favor. Its form should say that you are a person who is serious about writing, attentive to detail, careful, businesslike, mature and a good writer.

The editor, in most cases, has no idea who you are, if you are nine or ninety, sowing your oats or going to seed, fat or flat, Ivy League or bush league, active or radioactive. And she probably doesn't care. What is wanted is a professional writer who will produce an article that will sell more copies of that editor's publication, an article that is accurate, well written and submitted before or when it is due. Your letter must reinforce your image of professionalism.

All the editor knows about you at the first contact is what can be seen and read in the query letter. That is the sum total of the clues the editor must decipher in deciding whether to give you a go-ahead. If the written message of that query is extraordinarily convincing, detracting visuals in the letter's form and appearance may be overlooked. But if there are enough clues that the writer isn't professional, at least in intent, doubts will rise. Too many doubts and the query will end up in the reject pile, even though the idea posed may be very good.

If the publication doesn't appear in *Writer's Market*, it means either that it has folded (and definitely isn't the place to query) or, simply, it isn't listed. Check first to see if it is still sold on a regular basis, and if so, secure a copy and find the list of editors (usually near the table of contents), the address and other related information.

Query a current editor

Is it really that important that you send your query to a current editor? Consider a talk I had with the managing editor of a sports magazine—the third person in that position in thirty months. He had a rule of thumb in replying to queries or manuscripts that he felt was typical, in principle, of other editors he knew. If queries or manuscripts were addressed to the first editor, gone more than two years, they were kept in a box for some weeks, unopened, and were then switched into their own SASEs, a rejection note was inserted and the material was returned, unread. No SASE, it was dumped.

If the previous editor's name was used, since that person had departed only six months back, the queries were read as they arrived, but the manuscripts—which the magazine did not want without a previous query—were returned, unread, in about two weeks.

Any query sent to the current editor was read the day it arrived and acted upon promptly. His logic was simple: If the person hadn't read the publication for two years, which was implied by the use of the first editor's name, the writer had no idea of the substantial changes the magazine had undergone. Even the use of the previous editor's name indicated that the writer was violating a commonsense requirement for professionals: They must keep current on the publications and their top staff. Using the wrong name meant that it had been at least six months since the writer had checked the publication. Even if he had flipped through a more recent copy, he hadn't had enough sense to see who was the current editor to whom he should be writing!

Also use the editor's right name. Calling the editor by the wrong name isn't the brightest way to win favor. Petty? Perhaps, but you are a private and the editors are, at least, petty officers.

Querying by fax

Don't do this unless an editor tells you to, and don't count on that happening.

The best guide concerning the preferred querying means will be suggested in *Writer's Market* for your initial contacts, then any supplemental instructions given by the editor later. Unless it says otherwise, query by letter sent by regular mail.

Faxes are super when speed is desired, and in those rare situations where querying by telephone is called for, as mentioned earlier, then the fax will work nearly as well and the reason for its use would be understood by the editor. Otherwise, there is little urgency when suggesting an article that must usually wait two to three months to see publication, plus some three weeks or so in preparation, after the editor's query reply. A couple of days more isn't that critical. Your inquiry doesn't get lost in the flurry of faxes, it isn't read (and rejected) by every intermediary through whose hands the fax passes and the letter has a far more professional, cleaner and easier-to-read appearance than any fax.

That does not mean, however, that there may not be times when the fax is by far the best way to convey information to the editor; though in the usual process of researching, writing and submitting, those times will be few:

• You may encounter information that would make your article much more timely or useful, though it would change the direction or thrust you had suggested in your query.

• You may suddenly get access to a true luminary in the field to interview, and that interview will likewise redirect the final copy.

• You may accumulate enough related information to create a box or sidebar to accompany the article.

Those are the kinds of situations where talking with the editor, by phone or fax, benefit the publication and help you better direct the words in formation.

If the information to be shared with the editor fundamentally alters the direction of the article or the philosophy or assumptions supporting it, or it results in considerable additional material to be boxed with or integrated into the text, check before proceeding. Consultation, by fax or phone, makes the most sense when the end result will be an article clearly different from that posed. Rather than shocking the editor and receiving back, "Sorry I can't use this piece. It's not what you proposed in the query," suggest to the editor that you can provide the article as described in your query or there is the possibility of coming at it from a different way, or whatever, as you expound on the alternative direction and why that has become possible. Then a fax is a godsend, particularly if telephoning isn't your forte, you think better in print and you'd like a response in writing.

The danger is in overdoing it, interrupting the editor for every new fact or slight deviation. A few editors like to get involved as articles evolve, and will generally tell you so in your query response. But the overwhelming majority leave the work, decisions and wordplay to you, excepting to receive the result of your best effort in a final manuscript on or before the deadline.

Querying by e-mail

In the not-too-distant future, most queries may well be sent by e-mail, as manuscripts will be attached to files and mailed through the ether. But we're not there as this book is being written, with some notable exceptions: They are the computer magazines and a few daring avant-garde souls who have leapt ahead of both the horse and the cart.

Once more, let the annual *Writer's Market* direct you. It tells who wants to find queries and correspondence in their incoming computer mailboxes and who wants to be contacted through the postal services. Since its listings change each year, the growing number of Internet users for regular communication will be noted.

If an editor is e-mail savvy, uses the Internet regularly and isn't adverse to your using that media to make contact, then once the query has yielded a go-ahead (the very times when it is smart to correspond by fax or phone), you could as well use e-mail.

In fact, you are more likely to be benefited by the Internet informally than as a regular correspondence tool. If you drop into topic-related user's groups, you can do quick research. If the groups are publishing or publisher related, while you chat, exchange information or ask/answer questions, you will likely encounter an editor doing the same. That often leads to opportunities to exchange ideas, which in turn leads to query possibilities, whether by e-mail or the more traditional USPO means. Don't abuse this, though. And remember that as you talk by typing, your writing, spelling and grammar are being analyzed by a person to whom such things are lifeblood-linked!

Querying by phone

A few publications in *Writer's Market* prefer telephone queries, while most list phone numbers with their addresses. There's only one time when initiating your contact with an editor (who didn't specifically request it) by telephone makes much sense: if you have an item so hot or a situation so timely you need an immediate response.

Do you have the inside track to the top revolutionary about to overthrow a hostile country? Did you just receive a special visa to a nation that will open up its borders to outsiders in three months? Is a paper about to be released that will reveal the cure to herpes?

I found myself in a similar though less dramatic situation some years back when I had to use the telephone. To my surprise I wound up with nearly $1,500 in speculation go-aheads, all but one of which turned into paid articles. I joined a gold-hunting expedition to the Oriente section of Ecuador on the headwaters of the Amazon (actually the tributaries of the Napo River), and in the long shot that we didn't find gold and I survived, I wanted to back up my investment with offsetting articles. The group was leaving in ten days!

So I called a men's fraternal magazine and got story leads in Colombia and Ecuador. A travel magazine wanted an item about Bogotá and a consortium of three religious magazines went together on a piece about missionary work in Ecuador in which each church was taking part. And a camping journal wondered about backpacking in the foothills of the Andes.

I simply told each that I was headed that way, spoke Spanish like a native (a native with a very odd vocabulary and gringo syntax—in an area where most of the "natives" knew only Indian tongues!) and could handle my own photography. They provided the subjects, letters of introduction and bountiful goodwill. The church group even advanced $100—a true and unrequested act of faith. Friends called it a miracle.

There was a hook, though. Each publication was located in the greater Chicago area where I then lived, and I had time to visit most of the editors in person, after the phone contact, to sound out the specifics about what they wanted in the overseas report. In all, quite the reverse of most query approaches.

Why doesn't querying by phone usually work? Because most editors hate it. They are busy, resent being distracted, prefer to work on paper or in print and aren't looking for phone buddies. The best a writer gets even if the editor is available and courteous is, "That sounds interesting. Write me a query and let me look at it!"

There are some advantages to the kind of formality and the safe distance a query letter provides. Some people simply don't communicate well by phone. They stammer or beat around the bush, they are intimidated by the editor's name or position or they may have a voice that grates or dances over the octaves. Or they may be the type of people who think before writing but don't before speaking, or think so slowly or fully they sound simpleminded to those who don't know them.

That may be you. You might be a genius at the keyboard, a word jock of the highest paint, but sound like a lunatic on the phone. Or just like the editor's ex-husband, that no-good . . . Why take the risk unless there's no other choice?

Your purpose is to draw the editor's attention to an idea you want to write for her publication. A phone conversation may well distract from that purpose, where a well-written letter wouldn't.

Alas, once you know the editor, or the editor initiates the call, these factors become far less important.

Querying in person

Fortunately, this is impossible in most cases. The editor works in New York City or Chicago and you live in Tulsa, Rome or Burlington Junction.

Even if the publication is within an easy drive, the best selling chemistry takes place on the page, and the personalities between the idea and print are of little importance. So why put your person in the way of your prose? The idea you want to sell must first catch the editor's interest, and your subsequent written treatment of that topic is what matters. The editor is busy; you are eager to sell. If you pop into the office with an idea half formed, or even fully formed, and the editor isn't ready to consider it, you cannot relive the moment that didn't work. A query letter, on the other hand, sits around until the person you must impress is in a receptive mood. Or so you hope.

Even if you live down the street from the top dog, how does this substantially differ in pitfalls just described or from calling a query on the telephone? What can the editor say but send me a written query so I can give it full consideration?

What if you meet an editor at a cocktail party, some less formal gathering, or at a writers conference? Shake hands, be friendly, and if it's appropriate and convenient, give the beleaguered soul your business card and ask if it would be OK to send a query by mail during the coming week. If the editor asks more about your query idea, give the highlights. With the world full of would-be writers, most gestating an unwritten novel that would be a best-seller (no doubt an autobiography, in painful detail) if they just had a chance, editors are regularly approached by outsiders wanting them to provide that opportunity. So it's likely he will have forgotten who you are by the next morning.

Also, what if your prose is magic but your appearance (like your phone voice) is poison to the editor? You're too tall or too short, too warty or too smooth, too young or too old, a buffoon or not funny enough. Worse yet, you may look exactly like the editor's twin brother, the one who got the looks and stole his way to fame. Once seen, you are pegged for life—and your words remain unbought.

Better not to be seen at all, except in sparkling, witty, clear phrases certain to pull thousands of excited new readers to the publication. Then, if a meeting transpires, you have the saving grace of being part of the editor's success. Funny how much better you will look then!

The purpose is to get in print. Send your query letter to the editor's office. That will restore his faith in native, untapped genius.

Two final reasons not to query by phone or in person

What if the editor says, "great, bar no expense," during the personal or phone interview, and you invest precious time and funds to produce a masterpiece, rush back to the office to deliver the gem and that eager visionary says, "No, I'm sorry, I don't recall that discussion. . . ."? Or the editor has left the publication, and the replacement, busily wiping the slate, can't find anything on the desk about such a commitment. Such tales are well rooted in freelancing mythology. Writing for paid publication is a business. Keep the queries and commitments on paper, from inception to completion.

You also need some written proof of your query and go-ahead to justify your related income tax deductions, whether the piece is ultimately bought or rejected. More on that later.

Submitting several different queries at once

Keeping ten queries active at a time might be a sensible early goal, knowing that at best about a third might bring first-response go-aheads. The rest of the queries sent will be rejected outright or, rarely, after follow-up correspondence. Rarer yet, sometimes you will receive no reply at all from the query.

That 3:10 ratio is quite optimistic at the outset and pertains solely to editors to whom you have yet to make a sale. Once you have sold to an editor, while the querying process is the same, your expectation of a positive response should be much higher—assuming your first selling experience was agreeable to the editor. Given a choice of querying an editor to whom you have sold or a new editor, favor the first over the second, filling in your quota of ten with the latter.

Simultaneous submissions

A more difficult question refers to the number of the same queries—the exact same, word-for-word, or even written somewhat differently but promising the same copy about the exact same topic—that a writer can send simultaneously to different editors.

Again, a query is, in legal terms, an offer to sell a specific item to a publisher. You can sell an item as often as you wish. The problem comes when the purchaser wants to buy it with some degree of exclusivity. If that purchaser wants to buy "all rights," it can be sold only once. If "first rights" are the buyer's wish (as it usually is in the magazine world), the article can only be sold to that buyer for initial use, and then resold again and again, without restrictions, for reprint use after it has appeared in print on that editor's pages. In either case, you cannot initially sell the same rights simultaneously to different publications.

That's fine, you reply, but I know that if I query five times, I'll be lucky to get one nibble, much less two bites, or sales, so what's wrong with shortening my odds and speeding up the process?

That's why, on the surface, the question is a hard one to answer. You can send the same basic query out five times and take your chances. Low-selling beginners and short-term freelancers have been doing it for decades.

But it is risky—and skirts too close to being unethical. Say you do find the golden egg and have three hungry editors panting after the same gilded shell. Each wants that copy on her pages. And each buys first rights.

You could throw your future to the winds, write it once, make two copies, send all three out and pray nobody notices. Pulling that off unnoticed is about as likely as winning the lottery undetected. Editors keep a close eye on other publications in their broad fields. They or someone on their staff will notice, or a reader will spill the beans. If all three use the item, you will likely have three very angry editors. They may sue, at least to recover what they paid you. They'll surely add you to those dreaded no-buy lists they keep of freelancers who have stiffed or otherwise offended them. You've blocked yourself out of every market that editor works forever. And those editors always end up editing the very publications you have your heart set on cracking.

You could tell each of the three about your dilemma and offer to sell it to the highest bidder. Editors love blackmail and rush to outbid their colleagues to add a rookie to their freelance stables.

You could respond to the editor on whose pages you most want to appear, ignoring the others, pretending their replies never arrived and hoping they don't notice when you don't send in the copy they are eagerly awaiting. That presumes the first editor buys your article and the other two don't add you to their lists. A lesser lottery.

Or you could write three clearly distinct articles, one precisely as promised in the query, the other two distinctly reslanted so while the same subject is covered, it reads, looks, feels, smells and sounds differently. Then take your chance that all three editors buy their versions of what they thought they were going to get. This is the best of a bad lot of choices.

It makes so much more sense just to list the publications in order, as determined by your feasibility study, and approach the editors one at a time until it is sold.

Or to approach the subject at the outset from three clearly different angles, create feasibility studies for each and write queries that make each of the angles irresistible, each again sent to the publications in order.

Selling the same basic article simultaneously to more than one editor who buys on first rights simply isn't worth the risk. They'll find out. As hard as it is to imagine, editors have friends. Other editors may be old college colleagues or next-door neighbors, and their staffs talk to each other. When each becomes aware that you have queried another and then sold them both the same copy, you will suffer. The key to your long-range success is culling good relations with editors, both through excellent research/writing and responsible marketing.

The exception: limited distributions

You can query about the very same words, however, when the publications queried do not overlap on distribution and rights.

For example, many newspapers publish weekly magazines that are distributed in or with the newspaper, usually on Sunday. Their distribution ranges are normally about one hundred miles. Since the magazines prefer to be queried (unlike the specific sections of the newspaper itself), it's perfectly acceptable to query the newspaper magazine editors in, say, Seattle, Kansas City, New Orleans, Atlanta and Boston simultaneously. If all five editors say yes, bingo!

In-flight magazines are in the same category. You can either query or simultaneously submit to those that do not overlap each other.

The same with regional and religious magazines. The editors of religious publications believe, probably accurately, that their readers are already followers of the faith. So they don't care if the same material appears in publications of other faiths. Thus if you could find a topic of equal interest to the Baptists, Methodist, Catholics and Druids— God knows what that would be—then go to it. But if there are three

Druid publications, query or submit to one at a time.

The regionals are limited only by the extent of their regions. An article on the beauty of the name Portland could be offered simultaneously, with impunity, to regional magazine editors in Maine, Indiana and Oregon. But if the region is the Twenty Lakes, all of the publications overlap and compete with each other, so query one at a time.

It is imperative that manuscripts submitted simultaneously to magazines clearly state the words SIMULTANEOUS SUBMISSION. If necessary, you can either further delineate the breakdown at that point—such as "Unitarian copy," "Northwestern U.S. copy," or "Hawaiian airlines copy"—or you can explain that delineation in the text of the cover letter itself. As with all submissions or queries, an SASE should accompany the item sent.

What you can expect back when

Every good query deserves a response. The question is what kind of response you can expect and when.

Market listings usually indicate response times, which generally vary from a week to many months. Those times refer to manuscripts. Queries are usually answered much sooner, within a week to ten days. Even when an editor dallies, the delay is seldom as long as that indicated in *Writer's Market*. And when it is, the reason is often positive: The query had to be shared with other editors and is thus being seriously considered.

The type of response you can expect is very much related to the type and quality of query letter sent. A well-written, thorough, exciting query almost always gets a personal reply from an editor, whether that editor is interested or not. Even rejections to such queries often include an invitation to query again. That is logical, since a well-done query tells an editor this is a professional writer who may later have something valuable to offer.

Five kinds of query replies

There are five generic replies to a query letter.

The first is no reply. You don't hear back.

The second is a rejection: "It doesn't meet our present editorial needs," or something as coffer-crushing.

Neither is good news.

The next two are positive.

Mail the manuscript and a check will be sent, now or upon receipt, for its purchase.

Mail the manuscript on speculation—the editor thinks the final piece, once read, can be used, as is or with alterations—and if it is usable, a check will follow.

Sometimes there's a fifth reply, a kind of holding action. It says the article is being considered and the editor will get back to you soon. (There is usually a mammoth gap between your "soon" and the editor's.)

Rejections

An editor will often respond to a good query by specifying why the idea can't be considered at present: A similar piece is in hand or en route, it is too close to something recently used, the idea sits too far to the side of the readers' interests, the setting is outside the publication's main circulation, etc. The editor might suggest a different angle or slant, or that a history piece be set in a different time frame. The reward of a good query letter is that the editor notes your name and has you in mind, at least peripherally, for possible future purchases.

A sensible way to fix your desire and availability more firmly in that editor's mind is to follow a warm rejection to a query with another query on a different subject fairly soon, while your name is fresh. In the second query, also mention the topic of the first, in case it's the topic and not your name the editor recalls.

Having said that, a mimeographed rejection to your query doesn't necessarily imply the query was poorly written. Some editors simply do not send personal notes. You will learn who they are, though hopefully your other queries will generate so much work that rejections in general will diminish and the impersonal denials will become sad memories of an early writing past.

An impersonal response isn't a foolproof gauge as to the worth of a query. Sometimes even poor queries draw personal replies, usually negative in result though harmless enough in tone. An impersonal response does say something, however. If you receive nothing but an unbroken string of faded, general rejections, take a hard look at what your queries are saying, how they are saying it, what they look like and where they are being sent. Then ask yourself if the ideas you are trying to market aren't so limited in interest that there are too few readers to justify their being used.

Another thought about rejections is so obvious it should remain unstated if it weren't so frequently violated: If an editor says no, don't try the same query with a different editor at the same publication. Good ideas are often discussed at regularly scheduled meetings of the general editorial staff. If your idea reached that level, then was rejected, the second editor would naturally follow suit. Even worse, there is usually just one editor who handles the type of manuscript you propose, so if you've already addressed that editor the first time, then tried another, the second submission will likely filter back to the first editor on the second attempt! In short, the only way to sell that publication would be for the first editor to expire, flee or retire, and it seems to be a rule in granite that any editor who rejects a query will never do any of the three, while editors who accept queries have the permanence of vapors.

Standard rejections. The form standard rejections take is usually the blandest possible. "Sorry, this does not meet our present editorial needs. Thank you for considering us. Good luck in placing it elsewhere." Or something similar. Paltry stuff for your investment of time, brainpower, postage, research and hope. Still, it's better than writing the entire manuscript, then receiving the same unkind message.

Rejections with teeth. If you get a rejection with teeth, you probably earned it. I recall one from my own Dark Ages that says it all. I had tried to hawk a humor short about motion sickness to an in-flight magazine. Not a surplus of brightness there. (Because it was humor and a short, I sent the manuscript directly, without a query.) I asked the editor to imagine a passenger just settling in after a roller coaster takeoff, barf bag in one hand, magazine in the other, launching into a laugh-filled ditty about the galling horrors of air sickness! I forget the editor's exact response. Some of his words weren't in my writing vocabulary. "Nausea" was mentioned repeatedly, "wit unfettered by common sense" was suggested and there was a strong hint his competitor's magazine was the perfect place for such a revolting topic.

Similar language can be expected when you try to pawn pornography to church journals, drinking ditties to *Jack and Jill* and life-after-death pieces to retirement monthlies.

Go-aheads

The go-aheads are much more fun to read. "Let's see what you have. . . ." is a common reply, scribbled in fourth-grade Palmer at the bottom of a query. Or "Send me the article on speculation." Never "This is the best query I've ever read. How can the manuscript be anything but better? $3,000 enclosed. Rush copy—we are holding the next issue. How can we ever thank you for picking us?"

Actually, positive replies are often as bland as the rejections—with reason. You query about a new baseball bat being proposed for *Slugger Magazine*. The editor reads your letter. He likes the idea and is enthused by the query. He thinks you can send accurate, well-written copy soon. But he doesn't know you. He doesn't want to promise too much in case the manuscript is unusable. He's hoping for a home run but has received too many strikeouts to allow himself to get too enthused. He encourages you to finish your research and write the text for his publication, but he doesn't want to risk cash on the outcome. Go ahead, he says, and he'll look at the result—no promise to pay in advance. He has a thousand reasons why: factors beyond his control, the magazine may fold, he may be flooded by better copy from his regular suppliers, the topic may appear in a competitive journal, his stockpile is filled. And so on.

Don't let the blandness bother you. Most editors write the names and topics of their go-ahead responses in their calendars under the months they plan to use the copy, if usable. They might give ten go-aheads for eight slots, knowing that one will probably fall by the wayside—Did the freelancer die? Did an enemy write the query? Did she get cold feet so close to publishing victory?—and another may have photo difficulties or the facts or quotes may prove tougher to get than expected. The editors expect to use your copy, have a spot for it and will be just as unhappy if you do not get it in on time, about the subject promised and written to the needed level. Unhappy is too bland: Most will be irked, or just plain angry, at your leaving them with a copy hole. (Good luck with your next query to that editor!)

In other words, a go-ahead almost always results in a sale if you keep up your end of the bargain—do the research and writing at your own expense. Don't worry about the query response's wording. Respond as if it were delivered by a public crier and a corps of buglers. Imagine the editor desperate to use your best words. That's not too far from the truth.

Legalities. There's another problem too. If an editor says, "Yes, send me your article about ratfish. I'll pay $500 for it," that editor has sealed a contract. The three elements of contract—offer, acceptance and consideration—have been met. Even if you send in a manuscript that stinks to the next county, it *is* about ratfish and on time, so you are due $500.

Of course, getting the $500 may be a task, but legally you are in the right. The editor made no stipulation about quality or acceptance contingent upon approval of the text.

That hasn't gone unnoticed by editors. Their first words they heard from their publications' attorneys were, "Don't say *yes!*" Especially when they can say, "Let me see it," and get you to do the work at no risk, then make a decision when the final product is in hand. Unfair? It's certainly unequal, yet beginners trying to break into print and establish themselves as reliable wordsmiths who can produce for publication must accept the reality. Fairness here is for academics and lawyers. Bland go-aheads from queries, to be prepared and submitted on speculation, are the reality for newcomers.

Kill fees. There is a median point between a purchase and a rejection. Some editors pay "kill fees" for copy that is assigned but not bought, to somewhat offset the cost of the writers' energy and labor and to allay their disappointment. (The copy and illustrations still belong to the writers, who can sell them as is or modified to any other editors, after querying.) Kill fees are usually for one-third to one-half the expected payment, or from $400 to $600 on a $1,200 assignment. Rarely, this is also paid to freelancers working on speculation, particularly if they regularly write for that editor.

Suggestions by the editor. Often enough an editor will provide specific suggestions, even instructions, in his query reply about what you should include in the article.

That's excellent news because it shows extra involvement and enthusiasm by the editor, indicating a likelihood that the piece will indeed be used if it is researched and written well enough.

Do what the editor says—or, if that's impossible, explain why. The editor is probably telling you your angle needs some redirection or beefing up. Or that the readers seek a particular type of information and it is imperative your article address it. Look upon such suggestions as conditions: "If you can include this or that and the piece is otherwise written to my magazine's level, I can use your article on my pages."

What do you do in each case?
No reply

Wait two months (unless it says longer in the current *Writer's Market*). If you haven't heard after sixty days, dig out (or call up on your computer) a copy of your original query, and make a copy of it. Then write a short note to attach to that copy to mail to the editor. The note contains three points:

1. "A copy of the query attached was sent to you on _____."
2. "I haven't heard back. Perhaps the query got lost in the mail." Fat chance, but you can't tell the editor (a) you think he gave your idea to his cousin to write, cutting you out of the loop, (b) he's a dimwit who wouldn't know talent if it afflicted him, (c) he's a candidate for a pine suit when you get the word to *your* cousin, or (d) anything else similar that will make him eager to welcome you into the fraternity of preferred, high-paid regular contributors to his pages.
3. "Is the idea still as exciting now as it was then?" You did write the query and you'd still like to write the article for big bucks, so you might as well ask.

A number of things could have delayed the response. The editor intends to write back but the query got buried, mislaid or delayed in another office. Or the reply arrives the day you send your letter. Or the editor is no longer the editor, and the newcomer hasn't had time to reject what the old editor didn't. Or the publication has folded and you're not keeping your *Writer's Market* current with the *Writer's Digest* updates. Alas, it's usually the last. Like your dead uncle Mort, dead publications don't write back.

Wait for another month after your query copy and note reach the editor. If you still haven't heard, the publication might as well have folded, for you. Write it off. Go to the next lucky editor on your list.

Wouldn't a phone call be faster? Only if the publication hasn't folded. But it's nowhere as efficient. The editor probably (try 10:1 odds) won't know who you are, what you queried about or where the query is. If he even bothers to look for it, he's not going to be in a very positive mood to give you the nod you wish. I'd send the copy of the query with the note just described. If you still don't hear in a month and you want to try to rouse that deadbeat one last time, then call. (Then good luck getting paid on time, even if you get a go-ahead and a buy!)

A rejection

Idiots. Go to the next market on your list and query it. No, do not rewrite the query and try the rejecter again. Second rejections are usually much, much stronger, including specific reasons why the editor gleefully turned you down the first time. Aggravated editors tend to remember you longer too. Slip away quietly. That way you can bedevil the rejecter sooner with a different query about a different subject!

An assignment

For a newcomer? About as likely as that fabled money tree growing in somebody's backyard. Sometimes the second time around, more often the third or later, when the editor knows you, has faith in your ability and punctuality and wants you in the publication family. Sometimes never.

On speculation

Now you're talking reality. Mail the manuscript on speculation, meaning that if the editor thinks the final piece, once read, can be used, as is or with alterations, a check will follow.

Holding

These can run the gamut, from highly likely to be approved but one of the key people is on vacation (or picking up a Pulitzer) to an indecisive no, a query simply too good to just flat out reject. I'd wait a month, then call and ask the editor if a decision has been made. Try to find out the manuscript's status and when you can expect a definitive answer. Is there anything more you can do to aid in its acceptance? Should you call again (suggest a date one week, several weeks, a month away), or will the editor contact you?

If accepted, when should you send the manuscript?

When you get a go-ahead from a query, the editor giving you the nod becomes a very important person to you. Unfortunately, you are far less important to that editor, who has a dozen articles in process plus other editorial worries, like query letter reading to find more ideas for future copy. The editor will remember your idea, maybe your name, but likely little more.

For that reason, query only when you think you can get the manuscript to the editor within a three-week period. That way, from the date you get the green light until the "package" is en route, there is a sufficiently short period of time for the editor to have it and you in mind, and, should it require some rewrite, there is still time to make alterations before publication.

Further, state in the query that the manuscript and attachments will be in the editor's hands within three weeks.

There is one major exception. When travel is required, query as much as six months in advance, telling the editor when you plan to leave and return. To the return date, add about three weeks, and promise to have the copy in the editor's hands by that date.

You've tried to convince the editor you are a professional by the content and appearance of your query, so extend that same professionalism to honoring time commitments. Do everything possible to get the copy in his hands within twenty-one days.

Yes, I have missed deadlines, but rarely. In each case, before the third week, I wrote or called the editor explaining why a delay would take place and when the copy would arrive—within ten days, maximum, of the earlier deadline.

I've had editors tell me they like receiving the copy so quickly. It gives them a chance to see the material while the idea is still hot. I think it results in many more sales, though there is no way to prove that. In my case, it also forces me to get to the writing quickly and to do a more thorough pre-query job of researching and annotating sources.

Querying abroad

For some experienced writers, selling abroad is quite lucrative, but for newcomers, the cost, time delays and lack of familiarity with the publications themselves usually make the venture unprofitable.

Canada is the exception, where the querying process is the same and one can easily find copies of both the magazines and newspapers in major U.S. libraries or well-stocked newsstands, making it possible to study the markets before querying. (To a lesser degree, the same holds true for Mexico.)

Overseas, your best chance of selling is to English-speaking publications where the editor must alter the slang and insert regional peculiarisms for local use. That is, unless you are truly fluent in another tongue and wish to query in that language, then translate your copy before submission.

Stamps are another difficulty. Other countries won't accept U.S. stamps to return your SASE any more than you would accept horseflies to carry cartage.

Sometimes you can buy stamps of other countries at their embassies or consulates, plus receive a list of current mailing rates. Otherwise, just include a self-addressed envelope with your query and explain your plight, relying on the editor's goodwill, and purse, not to reply if he isn't interested in the idea but to let you know if he wishes to see the manuscript, deducting the mailing costs from the final payment. If you hear nothing in sixty days, query elsewhere.

Querying abroad now and then just doesn't work that well, so let me suggest two other approaches, with emphasis on the second.

The first is to sell reprints overseas, pieces that have sold in the U.S. yet have enough appeal to interest readers anywhere. Those usually fall in the travel or general interest category, although specific trade or specialty items might well work too if you can find matching publications in the foreign markets.

If the resale takes place, fine. If it doesn't, it is a small gamble since there is little or no rewriting involved. The only expenses come from making a photocopy of the original, putting it in an envelope and sending it boat rate with a cover letter explaining where the item was previously used and when and that you are selling second or reprint rights. Mention why you have not included return stamps. It might cost you $1.50 for shipping and fifteen minutes to photocopy and address, on the long shot that it will be used abroad and pay from $25 to $350. Where photos are involved, include a list of available prints or slides, plus a copy of the appropriate caption sheets, and ask the receiving editor to please indicate which shots he would like to consider. If interested, the editor will reply by mail (snail or e-), fax or sometimes call. Then you send the photos agreed upon, and eventually the payment and the photos come back.

Yet there's an easier way.

There are sales houses that act as brokers between American writers and hundreds of markets abroad, some in English, many in foreign languages. They find the clients, make the sales pitch, handle the translations, reproduce the slides and pay you when you least expect it. That nets you about half the income you would have made had you done all the work of generating the sale yourself. It's a bargain at 50 percent.

Check the current *Writer's Market* under "Syndicates." Read the write-ups closely to make sure they sell to the types of publications you work. Then either query them or send a full manuscript, with information about illustrations, where the item has already been in print (if it has) and any rights others have purchased. Almost all of the syndicates listed are U.S. based or have local offices, so stamps are no problem, and you can use an SASE.

It's hard to imagine a sweeter sensation for a writer, new or veteran, than receiving a tearsheet or a magazine copy of her work in a language she's never seen written before—with a tidy check attached! Or to receive a quarterly payment sheet with foreign publications listed.

Sadly, there aren't many such syndicates, some years none at all, and a few that existed in the near past didn't reply to queries or acknowledge the receipt of manuscripts, even when contacted later. But most are attentive and quite frank. They reject more items than they accept, usually because the topics won't sell abroad or the photos are unusable.

Selling abroad? Concentrate on Canada, then perhaps Mexico, and when those sources are exhausted (or you are), check with the syndicates and/or head straight for the English-speaking magazine counterparts, particularly in Australia, New Zealand, South Africa and the British Isles.

Responses to submitted manuscripts

Let's say your query brought a positive reply. You send the manuscript. What can you expect back?

The editor's second letter, announcing the fate of your submission, can take far longer than the query response. Figure a month at the second step, often longer—though many editors do precisely the reverse and speed up the rate of communication.

Sometimes the editor will acknowledge receipt of the manuscript. More often it is assumed you know the process: The "package" you sent must be read by your editor, and often that editor's editor; the illustrations must be reviewed by the art or graphics editor; and so on. At the very least, the manuscript and attachments will be discussed again by the group at its regular meeting. The process takes time. Anxious time for you. Time to send other queries to other publications about other ideas.

Even then, after all the wait, the reply can be negative. At that point, though, you have a right to expect a personal note rather than a printed rejection without comments. (If no comment is included and you have the stomach for it, write and ask why the material wasn't used.)

Why would an editor reject your finished manuscript after giving you a go-ahead to your query? For one or many of six reasons: (1) you changed the subject, slant or angle in the final manuscript from what you promised or implied in the query; (2) you missed the deadline; (3) the elements used in the final manuscript were unacceptable: the facts, quotes, anecdotes or illustrations; (4) the final writing was too far below the publication's acceptance level; (5) the editor simply decided, after reading all of the copy available for use, that yours wasn't needed or wanted; or (6) for reasons beyond the editor's control (redirection of the magazine's editorial composition, a new editor with different content plans, a pending merger with another house), your manuscript was no longer usable.

The first four you can control. The last two are rare enough that you can't be concerned about them as you research and write your copy. Anyway, irresistible writing is the cure for (5)—so write irresistibly. There is no cure for (6).

Sometimes a rejection at this level isn't terminal. The manuscript is rejected but the editor suggests ways it might be altered and still be acceptable. Act on those suggestions and do the rewrite as indicated, to make the most of the time you've already invested researching and writing the original manuscript.

If the manuscript is rejected with a personal note, the reasons may sound limp: "no longer as vital a topic as before," "reduction of copy space," etc. The editor may be letting you down softly. The manuscript may not be nearly as good as your query led the editor to expect. It lacks the query's vigor, has too few facts or quotes, you took a different slant or changed the conclusions. The editor doesn't want to discourage you totally, but the copy can't be used as is. Worse yet, the editor doesn't think you can bring it up to an acceptable level. The rewriting, the time, the letters all take too much investment for too little certainty of yield. You blew it.

What do you do next? Query another publication, this time matching your query promise to what you have already written. Don't mention the first rejection. If the second editor then requests the manuscript, rewrite it to match the peculiar needs of that second publication and to rectify any shortcomings that led to its original rejection.

Put that first editor on hold for a while, to let the sour taste leave both of your mouths, before querying him again. Don't mention the first manuscript in any subsequent query. Start fresh. Just don't forget that hard-learned lesson: The manuscript you send the editor must always be as good as the one you promised in a good query!

CHAPTER SEVEN

Nonfiction and Fiction Book Selling

Book selling is different from article selling, though with nonfiction books one key element is shared in common with magazine articles: the query letter.

To sell your book, you must also propose a topic that others will pay to read, it must be written in usable style and prepared within a set time period and you must find a publisher willing to share your thoughts and words on paper.

The last is the biggest hurdle. Magazines are expensive enough to produce, but they come out often and your article is but a fraction of the elements that influence a buyer's decision. With a book, you are it: The book is sold once (if you're lucky) and what you say, and how you say it, carries the entire load. Publishers think twice, then twice again, before committing $15,000 or $50,000 or much more to putting book words to paper and running that through their erratic selling machines.

So finding a publisher willing to finance your dreams, or at least a hard month's labor, is the major hurdle. The rest is usually easy enough to bring into line.

There's a practical solution for sidestepping that hurdle: Become your own publisher. This suggestion panics almost everybody upon first hearing it. What do I know about publishing? Where could I get that kind of money? Who would buy the book from me? What will my friends, or even the critics, think when they discover I couldn't get a publisher and had to self-publish?

Brace yourself. Being your own publisher is not only the wisest choice you can make in many cases, it is sometimes the only choice— and it can be the most lucrative by far.

So let's talk book selling first, in the sense of selling your book concept to other publishers, from the New York giants to minuscule houses in tiny towns. Then let's focus on the two conditions where self-publishing is either a sensible choice prudent businessfolk would always consider or where it is the only, but a highly profitable, choice you'd be wise to rush to. In the last two cases, book selling means all but physically selling the books. You don't have to convince the publisher. You are it.

Nonfiction, fiction or faction?

There are three kinds of books: nonfiction, fiction and faction. Let's work backward.

Faction, in the simplest terms, is nonfiction using fictional techniques. It's the biography of King Tut, with dialogue and motivation and dreams, all invented or deduced from the few things known about the boy-king and his era. It's having Isabella chat with Ferdinand, in English, though not a word of their intimate conversation had been recorded. Or Truman Capote retelling the precise steps and thoughts of two hapless killers at a Kansas home in *In Cold Blood*. Truth, but not quite truth. Sold as nonfiction.

Fiction, by titles, comprises less than 10 percent of the books sold annually. It's an extremely hard market to crack, in part because novelists have the felicitous habit of living long and writing often. It's also an area where self-publishing is ill-advised. Thus, with the majority of the larger publishers dedicated to nonfiction only, that leaves but a small cadre of established publishers seeking one or a few new fiction writers a year to add to their stables.

Contrast that with the popular concept that "anybody can write a novel," a premise that far too many nonwriters attempt to prove. The few fiction-buying channels get clogged with boxes of prose, tons of dangling metaphors, torrents of flowing consciousness. It's hard for the good stuff to get through.

So selling fiction is largely relegated these days to finding an agent, reworking the initial copy to her suggestion and holding on while she takes the new prose on a footpath around the clogged submission highway. This doesn't mean that super writing may not escape the sludge pile, be rescued by a diligent junior reader and sent to an acquisitions editor. But it's unlikely, however electric the prose. So let's address the larger topic of selling fiction first, then offer a few suggestions, before moving to nonfiction, where sales chances are many times better.

Selling your fiction book

The traditional way to sell a novel is to write it, edit it into final form, find a directory to fiction markets and submit it according to the guide's dictates.

There are four such guides readily available in bookstores or libraries: the current *Writer's Market*, the current *Novel and Short Story Writer's Market*, *Literary Market Place* and Jeff Herman's *The Insider's Guide to Book Editors and Publishers*.

Most give two sets of instructions: (1) submit through an agent or (2) send three chapters of the finished manuscript with a synopsis and a cover letter.

Using an agent

Fiction editors prefer using agents because agents screen out the worst submissions either by insisting the writing be brought up to an acceptable submission level or by refusing to handle it. If the writer does produce text the agent thinks has buyability, the agent then approaches specific editors and firms that publish in that field. Unlike anxious novices, agents won't submit blushing erotica to Christian houses or romances to Scientific Press.

Finding an agent is much like finding a publisher, and often as slow. Unless an agent is suggested to you or a successful fiction-writing friend gives you a name and address, comb *Guide to Literary Agents*, either of *Literary Agents of North America*, or *Literary Market Place*, and compose a list of agents you think would best serve your interests.

Write a sharp letter that explains you are seeking an agent, what you want agented, as much as needed about you and your writing experience and that you have a manuscript you'd like the agent to sell.

It's perfectly ethical to send the same letter (and, later, manuscript) to many agents simultaneously. Only when one agrees to represent you and you are satisfied with the terms must you inform those still in the running that you are being represented by _____, and thank them for their consideration.

A model letter might look like the example on page 123. If you find an agent to represent you, simply follow his instructions since he is the negotiator for you with a buyer. He sells for you, for 10 to 15 percent of the sales price, deducted at the time the contract is paid, since contract checks are sent to the agent, who sends your percentage to you.

Selling your own fiction

Historically, most novelists sold their first books themselves. Agents then courted them to handle subsequent manuscripts.

The path is well worn and guided by common sense.

First go to the library and/or bookstore and note the name of every publisher who has recently released a book in the genre or field in which you write: suspense, western, science fiction, gothic. Check the guides mentioned earlier to see what they are currently seeking, then create your market list in preferred order, with the house you'd most like to be represented by first. Most common criteria are likelihood of the book seeing light soon, the advance and royalty, the publisher's prestige or power in the field and vigor in selling spin-off products and rights.

Then write a solid one- or two-page, single-spaced cover letter that tells the acquisitions editor what your novel is about, who would be interested in reading it, titles of other high-selling books like yours, how yours differs, what special knowledge or experience you bring to the research or writing, anything in your life that will enhance the salability of the novel or you, your desire to help make the book sell (book selling tour, radio/TV interviewing, book signings, etc.) and anything more you think will help the editor decide to at least request the full manuscript.

With the letter, you will submit three chapters of the manuscript (including the first, which is needed for table-setting and character introduction) and a one-page, single-spaced synopsis, if necessary.

The short cover letter looks remarkably like the one sent to secure

(Your Name)
(Your Address)
(City, State ZIP)
(Your Phone/Fax)
(Date)

Uran Agent
123 Fourth Avenue
New York, NY 10017

Dear Agent (or Agency):

Some fifteen years back I led a gold hunt into the Upper Amazon region of Ecuador's Oriente, on the eastern slopes of the Andes Mountains. The group divided into sections: my advanced party of eight, followed several weeks later by a supply unit of ten. We left Quito to cross the top of the Andes by bus and set up a supply depot in the last inhabited outpost on the Napo River, Coca, from which we climbed the Paushi-Yaco and Chapano Rivers into an area never entered other than by savage Auca Indians.

I led the first group, and that is the basis of the novel I have written. Alas, the leader in my book isn't me but rather a treasure hunter named Greg Scott, who is almost 8″ taller, 30 pounds heavier and 29. Link Hudder is also in the group: black, wiry and terrified of the venomous green (coral) snakes, the cayman and the stray piranha, yet he emerges as the strongest of the followers. Barraga Lopes, the tracker, dies the second day after the final camp is built. The question is why. Who will be next? And can the group survive until the supply party arrives—if it arrives?

Called *Death on the Amazon*, the book shares adventure at its toughest, then survival when humankind is forced to pit wit and strength against a peril even greater than an already hostile nature. I have enclosed an outline, a synopsis, a brief biography and copies of the first three chapters. I hope they will encourage you to want to read the entire manuscript and place it for sale with the best publisher in the suspense/adventure field.

Respectfully,

(Your Signature)

cc: enclosures

an agent since they are the two most common ways of achieving the same thing: getting your fiction read, then in print. Yet the direct submission requires unique inclusions, as the example on page 125 shows.

Sometimes there is so much other business needed in the cover letter—a detailed explanation of a complicated plot, a clarification of how you know the intricate knowledge needed, why the book would sell and so on—there is too little room to properly give an overview of the book. Then you need a one-page synopsis so the buyer has a straightforward summary or explanation to use to sell the rest of the editors at the publishing firm.

Some send the cover letter, three chapters and synopsis (if needed) to one house at a time, period. Some send to many publishers, particularly if the guides say they will consider simultaneous submissions. The choice is yours.

Then, if one or many editors ask to see the full manuscript, send it off, with the simplest of notes: "Here's the full manuscript of _____ , as requested. Please send me the good news as quickly as possible!" Be sure to have your name and address prominent on the text and note so the editor knows where to rush the magic words!

What do you do if an editor offers to buy? Enthusiastically thank her and ask to see the contract. Or enthusiastically thank her and ask for the names of the three best agents she works with. Pick one, send a representation request letter with a copy of the "buy letter" from the

(Your Name)
(Your Address)
(City, State ZIP)
(Your Phone/Fax)
(Date)

(Fiction Editor's Name)
(Position, Publishing Firm)
(Address)
(City, State ZIP)

Dear _____ (Editor's Name):

Some fifteen years back I led a gold hunt into the Upper Amazon region of Ecuador's Oriente, on the eastern slopes of the Andes Mountains. (Why me? I'm fluent in Portuguese and Spanish, can count in Tupi and have three degrees in Latin American Studies or related fields.) The group divided into sections: my advanced party of eight, followed several weeks later by a supply unit of ten. We left Quito to cross the top of the Andes by bus and set up a supply depot in the last inhabited outpost on the Napo River, Coca, from which we climbed the Paushi-Yaco and Chapano Rivers into an area never entered other than by savage Auca Indians.

I directed the first group, and that is the basis of the novel I have written. Alas, the leader in my book isn't me but rather a treasure hunter named Greg Scott, who is almost 8″ taller, 30 pounds heavier and 29. Link Hudder is also in the group: black, wiry and terrified of the venomous green (coral) snakes, the cayman and the stray piranha, yet he emerges as the strongest of the followers. Barraga Lopes, the tracker, dies the second day after the final camp is built. The question is why. Who will be next? And can the group survive until the supply party arrives—if it arrives?

Called *Death on the Amazon*, the book shares adventure at its toughest, then survival when humankind is forced to pit wit and strength against a peril even greater than an already hostile nature. I am sending the first chapter plus two others to give you a sense of the tension and fear. The final draft is completed, of course, and can be sent for full review as soon as you ask.

The Amazon forest may be slowly disappearing but its vicarious appeal for readers of all ages remains, though there have been few novels with it as a setting in the past decade. What distinguishes this story is that it's 80 percent factual, I lived it and as a professional speaker I'm ideally trained to help in any promotional way, if needed.

Finally, my writing background is fairly extensive, though this is my first novel. Starting as a newspaper reporter, I have subsequently sold 1,600+ articles and written 13 published books, all nonfiction concerning writing, speaking and entrepreneurship. I'd gladly send copies or clips at your request; a list of the books and a summary of recent articles are appended.

Respectfully,

(Your Signature)

cc: enclosure

publisher, and see if the agent will represent you in this transaction—and presumably in a hundred more such transactions in the future. Therefore, choose the agent carefully since you enter the arrangement in a favorable position.

Why would you "give away" 10 to 15 percent of your money by having an agent do what you could probably do yourself? Because he'll likely get you far more than that back in advance and royalties and position your book stronger for ancillary buys, and you have an agent for later sales.

Selling your nonfiction book

Nonfiction books are by far the most sought and, for freelancers, the easiest to sell. While the potential profits are greater by self-publishing (as are the risks) in the how-to area, what usually scares most writers into the hands of the standard publishers are all of the things that must be done after the book is researched and written, like the production (editing, typesetting, layout, illustration, bidding, printing, binding, ISBN and twice as much more) and the promotion—getting bookstores and libraries to get the book in circulation, plus reviews, shipping, billing and so on.

That's where most writers opt to let a publisher—a giant house in New York City or a tiny, one-book shop in Solvang—take over. The relationship is, on the surface, simple: You write, rewrite if needed at the editing stage, prepare the index and make yourself available to be interviewed by Leno or Letterman. The publisher does the rest.

When (if) the book sells, you will receive royalties of 6 to 15 percent of the retail price (though some publishers pay only on net, which means about half of that retail price). Sometimes the publisher will pay you part of those royalties in advance, then nothing until the sales catch up. If the book sells well but gets dated some years later, you may be asked to update the pages and do the indexing again, and with huge luck, the talk shows once more.

The publisher will keep at least 85 to 94 percent of the book's price for having produced and promoted your book, plus having gambled money on the chance that your work would be sufficiently profitable.

In terms of royalties, it matters little whether the book is a novel or nonfiction, except that advances on novels are usually lower and slower to receive.

The toughest hurdle you must scale is getting the publisher to agree to handle your book. You aren't alone in opting to have a company do the production and promotion. Some houses have hundreds of packages, proposals or actual new manuscripts arrive weekly, all shouting for acceptance. Most houses publish a few or a dozen new books annually. Even the largest firms, publishing several hundred books, rejected several thousand to find their selections.

Having said that, they would fold if people like you didn't write books for them to publish. They need you as badly as you need them. You simply must learn to speak their language and provide them with salable items.

Yet you are a new name, a new risk to them. They will judge you on what you send, the thought behind it, the obvious professionalism, how it reaches them, sometimes your expertise or previous writing output and always on how your book will increase their profit lines.

So it is imperative that what you send looks professional, is clear and clean, is thorough and believable in what it promises and answers every question the publisher would ask before saying yes. Questions like the following:

- Precisely, what is your book about?
- Who would read it?
- Why would they buy it?
- Where would they use it?
- What else is available like your book?
- How does your book differ from other, similar books already available?

What follows is a straightforward process that will help you answer those questions, quickly and directly, then prepare a submission for a publisher that will compete with veteran book writers vying for the same favorable nod, royalty advance and talk show seat.

Query letter

The query letter sent to the book publishing editor is similar to a magazine query, except it is two pages long instead of one. You need two to get the business done, but no more than two. Anything else can be included as attachments (like the three items following—a synopsis, a table of contents or outline, a reference/resource sheet).

What must you do on those two pages? One, tell what the book is about. Two, tell why *you* should write it. Three, identify what other books are currently on the market (or soon will be) that will compete with yours in sales. Four, if there are other books, explain why yours will outsell them. And five, show by the stellar writing and firm grasp of English and its writing requisites that you can in fact write several hundred pages of salable, readable prose.

The query letter is a sales letter. Here you are selling two things: the idea your book would develop and you as its champion and writer. So the letter must bring that idea alive, make it appealing, convince the editor that a book about it would be both profitable and valuable and that you can explain and discuss that idea engagingly for several hundred pages.

Sometimes the two pages are so full of other, necessary things that the space available to sell the idea is insufficient. That's when you must add a one-page synopsis—editors feel that if you can't do it in a page, you still don't have a handle on your topic. Include at least a paragraph about the book topic in the query, then refer the reader to the synopsis attached. About half the time synopses are needed. The rest of the time there is space in the query itself to make the topic and you clear and wanted.

As for why you should write the book, explain your specific credentials. (If the book is academic or professional, you may need to include a dossier or resume with your academic or professional qualifications in addition to highlighting the most important in the query itself.) If you have nothing that would commend you to write about this topic, dwell on your other writing, your interest and involvement with the subject or anything else that helps distinguish you as the potential author. If you flat out have no credentials beyond breathing, write so well and clearly about the topic in the query that it simply isn't an issue.

Other books currently in print, or soon to be, that will openly compete are financially important to the publisher. You must comb the bookstore shelves, the libraries nearby and *Subject Guide to Books in Print* to see what will be wrestling for the same buying dollar. Make a list of all such books, with the publisher and copyright date. Then read those books on the list to see why they were written (what working question do they answer?), their structures, the kinds of quotes and anecdotes they include, the depth they cover and how relevant they are to the state of the art in that field today.

While you are at the library, check *Forthcoming Books* to see which other competing books will see print in the coming six months. Add those to your list, and as they become available, read them too. (Contact the publisher and order a copy the moment the book is released. If it is within three months of the book's announced publication date, it most likely already exists.)

You should then be able to speak intelligently about all of the "competition." Focus on those books that will indeed attract the same kinds of buyers, and explain to the potential publisher in the query how your book differs and thus is likely to be bought instead of or in addition to the other book already released. For example, your book might be far more comprehensive, a summary far more useful in the field, or full of more recent facts and charts.

Incidentally, then make a list of those publishers and write the title and copyright date of each book after the appropriate name. The publishers listed most likely specialize in your field and are far more receptive to buying new books about it. Rank the houses from the most active to the least. That's where it makes the most sense to query, in that order.

A sample nonfiction book query is provided on pages 131–134.

Synopsis

As just explained, sometimes you need more space than the query letter offers to fully explain why and how the book is being written and what it's about. That's the chance to make your synopsis shine. If the editor finishes reading a synopsis and doesn't say (or at least think), "That's a book that should be written," go back and work on that synopsis until that happens.

On the rarest of occasions a synopsis-like page might be prepared— one page only, to accompany the query letter—that expands upon what your query promises.

For example, you may wish to approach a proposed book in two very different, and each complex, ways. You would develop the preferred approach in the query and the second in the page.

Or you may wish to create a series of three or four books but space doesn't allow any development of that concept in the query. So you sell the key book in the query and explain the broader concept, with a quick summary about each of the other books, in the extra sheet.

(Your Name)
(Your Address)
(City, State ZIP)
(Your Phone/Fax)
(Date)

(Appropriate Editor's Name)
(Position, Publishing Firm)
(Address)
(City, State ZIP)

Dear _____ (Editor's Name):

There is no area of publishing riper for growth, less risky or more profitable than niche publishing. For the past decade, computers have been developed to the stage (and dropped in price) to where home-based writers of any ilk can compose, edit, page-make and produce their own camera-ready text (or ready-to-use copy on computer diskette), then send it off for printing and binding. All that is missing is a niche marketing process, mostly done and tested before the first word of the manuscript is written, that gets the published items in buyers' hands (paid for in advance) the moment they arrive from the printers.

None of this is speculative, nor does a book need to be written and published that explains either the niche marketing or book production processes. My *Publishing to Niche Markets* is widely sold and much used for the marketing. For book preparation—everything from writing and camera-ready page preparation to indexing—Dan Poynter and Tom and Marilyn Ross have excellent books, with solid support books by Malcolm Barker on design and John Kremer on ancillary marketing.

What is missing is a *book of success stories* that tell how that was achieved, what specifically that means and—by implication—how the reader can follow suit.

Who would buy such a barn burner, your accountant asks? Promoted well and sold through both bookstores and lists of publishers, the market is huge. For starters, according to the *Occupational Outlook Handbook* of the Bureau of Labor Statistics (Spring 1996), there are 272,000 writers and editors in the United States. Their median salary ranges from $30,000 to 60,000. Those are people already earning money by writing, so for a few of them this book is more preaching to the choir. But for probably 80 percent, the whole idea of niche publishing is brand new—and the kinds of profits available, almost unbelievable.

Then there are the millions of people who "want to write a book" or do something by writing. We know too well that most of them should be heavily discouraged, but the flame burns nonetheless. Many will disregard anything that doesn't address novels, poetry or their diaries (or autobiography), but that still leaves a huge pool of wanna-be writers to whom this book will be an inspiration and a way to back into niche publishing.

The most obvious and best market is, paradoxically, publishers. Would they pay $20 to read a book about other publishers who are reaping 30 to 45 percent profit with little risk and no unsold books? You bet. They are the same folks already gobbling up *Publishing to Niche Markets*. How many of them are there? According to Dan Poynter, author of *The Self-Publishing Manual*, who based his findings on the *Books in Print* CD-ROM, 119,000 new titles saw light in 1995 (of which about 5,000 were reprints). There were 53,000 publishers in 1995, plus those who didn't release a book that year or who did but didn't use an ISBN. Of the 53,000 publishers, more than 52,500 were small houses. The most astounding number: There were 1,063,000 books in print in 1995.

So much for its marketing potential. Why don't I self-publish the book I'm proposing? Because it needs the widespread bookstore sales and library push a big house can provide and I can't. Having said that, I can provide an in-house mailing list of 28,000 writing-product customers that will help start a supplementary direct-mail marketing program, plus I can suggest the ways to reach the niched elements mentioned in the previous paragraphs.

The book I propose will run about 250 pages and will feature eight success stories from the wider niche publishing world, which has books as its core but other empire-building means disseminators also included, like audio- and videocassettes, reports (or monographs), CD-ROMs, computer diskettes, speeches, seminars and consulting. That is, the center of their success (typical of niche publishers) was the expertise they shared first in print and then by many related means.

If interested, I will gladly share the names and detailed bio sheets of the eight subjects who have agreed to let me write in detail about their publishing histories, the current state of their businesses, and where they project to go in the future. They will sign any legal release, within reason, that we create. (I have two more to consider should any of these turn out not to be fully cooperative.) Five are men, three are women. They range in age from 27 to 69. One has been in business less than a year, though they average 6.2 years in publishing, and one converted a firm after 29 years from broad, general markets to niche. They are fairly evenly distributed across the mainland United States (with one also in Hawaii).

Let me give you one example, in brief and with a few details slightly altered to preserve his anonymity at this point.

Eddie's father began a sod farm in Illinois 60 miles west of Chicago in 1947, which still exists. So Eddie grew up, with his five brothers, working for his father planting, cutting and transplanting sod. He went to the University of Illinois, received an M.S. in horticulture and decided in his spare time (while comanaging the farm with his older brother) to start writing articles for trade journals. Soon enough that led to general interest and home magazines, and by the time he reached one hundred publishing notches, he was regularly on TV as a gardening specialist, had a syndicated weekly radio show and was asked during one Q&A session where his book could be bought.

So he wrote that book—and published it. So much for turning sod! By the time the revenue passed $100,000, he had created a publishing company in his basement and was exploring the possibility of shifting his primary focus from gardening to the public to how-to books for those in the sod farm and agricultural produce trade. Within eighteen months, Eddie saw his revenues triple, reach a million dollars fourteen months later and now is approaching three million dollars two years after that. He has six employees, products in five supplementary media and just bought the sod farm from his brothers, two of whom will stay on (with their children) to keep it increasing its profits by a healthy 9.3 percent annually.

These are the touchpoints of success by niche publishing. The book would spend 20-30 pages giving the details, the thought process, numbers/costs/profit at every step and a lot more information about Eddie as well, about what makes him different, where his drive comes from, where he sees himself going, what process has brought him success and when he learned it.

There are no other books on the market about this topic, so the competition will come later. The only real question is whether you see this as a valuable addition to your line in the near future. If so, and you wish to know more details, please let me know.

Respectfully,

(Your Signature)

Table of contents/outline

In the query you tell the book editor what you're writing about, yourself and the competition, but the editor still has no idea how you propose to organize your material, if you do at all, nor to what depth you plan to go in writing (and researching) your book.

A table of contents to the rescue! There are two forms, the usual (seen in the front of almost all books) or an annotated table of contents created specially for the book editor. Why not use the latter? The only difference is that after each chapter heading you add a note (a sentence or several) explaining in greater detail what that chapter is about. Then the subsections, if any, make more sense. (You could continue doing that for the subsections too, if they need further elaboration.)

Make the table of contents as full as you must, but I'd stop before adding items you may not be able to provide or substantiate. In other words, full but lean. Much better not to speculate and include than try to sneak by ten or fifteen pages later out of pure gossamer.

Outlines are another way of showing where the book is headed and how it will be structured. A quick survey of some book editor friends: To a person they preferred the annotated table of contents. Then again, I have weird friends.

Reference/resource sheets(s)

All that is missing, from the editor's perspective, is where you are getting the facts, quotes and anecdotes to fill those empty pages. Voices in the night, mystical revelations, notes slipped back from the hereafter, even voices in the day make publishers betting many thousands of dollars on you more than nervous.

Better tell them where you're getting at least the major portion of your material—and if it's controversial, where you are getting your theories. That's done in a two-part guide.

The "references" part refers to all of the written sources you will use in compiling your book: other books, articles, case studies, reports, surveys and so on. Include about ten of the key written sources, in annotated bibliographical style. That means author or editor, title, publisher, date of publication and a sentence or two (or three) telling how you will use that material in your book.

The "resources" part, in this context, refers to all of the oral sources you will use, such as interviews, speeches, seminars, tapes, radio, TV and more. Some books use no oral material at all. But if you will be drawing from such sources, you might again limit the number listed to ten or so of the most important. Here you might list them by some annotated biographical style. An example:

> MARSHA FREEMAN is a dental SOPs (standard operating procedures) expert and author of *Standard Operating Procedures for Dentists* and *Standard Operating Procedures for Pediatric Dentists* who created the SOPs Dental Network in early 1997. I will interview Freeman about how SOPs can be used to increase a dental practice's value before and after a sale.

The final steps of the selling process are to put your package together and submit it, to one publisher at a time, to those houses that produce and sell books like the one you want to author. Both Jeff Herman's *The Insider's Guide to Book Editors and Publishers* and *Writer's Market* provide the names and addresses of the editors.

You will probably receive one of four generic replies. The first, a quick rejection. OK, thanks for not holding it half a year, even though the editor must be some sort of specimen not grabbing such a chance!

The second, a postcard confirming the book's receipt and telling you it has been sent to a strange province to be read and ruminated upon. Good news. Rumination precedes acceptance.

Reply three, a sort-of go-ahead, along the line of, "We like this idea and would like to see some sample chapters by _____, [usually several months off]—but we have some reservations." The reservations might be that you have too few valid examples to prove your book's thesis, or that there is too little material to produce enough salable copy, or that you want to spend half the pages talking about one aspect of the topic and the editor sees it best written from an entirely different article altogether. If you can satisfy his concern, go ahead. If some of his reservations are valid and others aren't and you want this publisher, try to negotiate or explain where you have the greatest difficulty. If the resulting book would mortify you, thank him and submit to the next editor.

The fourth response, "Looks good. Send some sample chapters by _____." No reservations (yet). About the best you get. Dig in and write three superb chapters. It makes sense to include the opening chapter because it explains what follows.

Number five doesn't happen: "Where have you been for the past thirty-five years? Your idea and presentation are so good I'm sending you the full $50,000 advance by Telex today. Get that golden prose to us some time this decade. Oh yes, if you need some more advance money, just call!"

If the editor likes the book, you are given a writing deadline and sometimes enough directions to find Philly in the dark. Or none at all. Plus a contract that stipulates when and how you get paid.

For example, a $5,000 advance for a new author is probably about average for a larger house. That is usually paid half when you sign the contract and half when you turn in the final corrected draft (which is several months after the first draft is due). If you don't submit any draft at all, you owe the first payment back. Some months later the book appears, you treat yourself to a victory supper and then you wait for your royalties. And wait. Until the sale of the books returns the advance to the publisher, who advanced it. Since you are paid two or three times a year, when there are additional royalties due you and the magic date arrives, the checks begin to appear. It's not uncommon to pass one or two pay periods without royalties, but when your first and second checks do arrive, they are often substantial. Alas, the bounty diminishes quickly and irreversibly downhill, unless a miracle occurs.

But why even mention that? You have a book in print! Congratulations. And thanks for writing it and sharing with the rest of us.

Publishing your own nonfiction general market book

The purpose of this book is to show you how you can sell your writing. In almost every case, that is to another person or firm, like an editor at a magazine or newspaper or even to a book publisher.

But there is a way to directly sell your writing, in a sense, to yourself, who in turn assumes the role of the firm. That is, you become the publisher. It is too costly and improbable to suggest that you create a magazine or newspaper just to make your own thoughts, ideas and information available in print. Both are major financial undertakings—the term may even be doubly appropriate considering their high mortality rate, particularly of late.

But it's indeed possible to become a book publisher with a modest investment of capital and more of sweat labor and industrious camera-ready production, then promotion.

Yet to do so is so complex it would take another book longer than this one to give you the details. The selling is easy. Ask yourself if you think your idea is worth buying. If you respond affirmatively, you've made a sale! It's everything else that begs instruction, such as how you make that sale work as a profitable, first-rate book.

So let me make a compromise on these pages. Let me provide a rough outline of when it makes sense (and cents) to publish your own book, show you the two most common paths to make that happen successfully, indicate several other books that will pick up in detail where I leave you with general instruction, share eighteen points you must consider before self-publishing, then let you decide to go with another publisher or do it yourself.

To successfully self-publish you must fully enact all three elements of book publishing: preparation, production and promotion. (Some suggest adding two more: patience and prayer.)

Many writers respond vigorously to that challenge because of the thrill of taking an idea and words and seeing them emerge in full book form, which they can directly sell.

More are probably attracted by the prospect of greater and quicker profits. Done right, the 6 to 15 percent royalties received from another publisher can be 25 to 60 percent of one's own book's retail price. The difference in income can be huge. It can also be in hand in weeks from the sale date, if sold by direct mail. (Usually half of your income is back within thirty days of receipt of your flyer.) And that income will continue to arrive almost daily, instead of the quarterly or six-month royalty payments once the advance has been satisfied.

On the other hand, there is no advance against royalties. In self-publishing the money flows the other way: You pay the book's production costs. Nor is there any guarantee that any profit will be made, or that you won't be out the entire cost of producing a book that never leaves your garage. There is a third element: that the time spent earning that income—the hours and energy invested producing and promoting the book—might not have been better put to writing another book or two to be sold by standard publishers.

In other words, risk. For standard self-publishing, the risk is relatively modest, the potential income is about the same (close to 25 percent), and the cost, from $3,500 to $8,000 (if you initially print 1,500–2,000 copies). For niche self-publishing, discussed in more detail later, the risk is very low (since you test your market first), the potential profit is very high (closer to 50 percent), and the cost, alas, is also very high (since you will sell almost all of your books by direct mail, which accounts for the higher expense).

What is the difference between standard self-publishing and niche self-publishing?

Standard self-publishing presumes that the bulk of your books will be marketed much like the regular publishing houses: either directly or through distributors to bookstores and libraries (normally at discounts of 40 to 55 percent). To that you will add some customized selling, such as back-of-the-room at seminars or speeches, at convention booths and so on. The greater the customized, low-discount selling or direct marketing to libraries, the greater your profit. How can self-publishers outsell the regular publishers? Through greater persistence, keener marketing, more customized outlets and lower overhead. But if the book isn't as good in content, value and physical appearance, any of those advantages will be quickly lost.

There are certain kinds of books it makes no sense to self-publish if profit is your driving motive, by either the standard or niched routes. Novels, children's books or poetry. Other kinds of books can be too risky in terms of cost versus profit. Those are books that must be widely seen (usually face outward on bookstore shelves) to be picked up by the curious. Books with general titles such as "How to Get Thin," "How to Grow Rich" and "How to Stay Young," bought by impulse buyers while browsing the bookstore. The problem with self-publishing them is that you can't guarantee your book will reach, much less be prominently displayed on, those bookstore shelves.

But some books shout to be self-published: mostly how-to books with clearly defined, accessible markets, which can be sold both directly and indirectly. All the better if they have a long shelf life.

There are perhaps a dozen solid books about self-publishing currently available in the library and bookstores. Three I think do the best job of giving the kind of step-by-step guidance we are providing in this book. The first two cover essentially the same ground, so either should explain well the full process of creating a self-published book, from the inception of the idea to reselling the remainders. Dan Poynter's *The Self-Publishing Manual* (Para Publishing) is the stronger of the two in marketing; Tom and Marilyn Ross's *The Complete Guide to Self-Publishing* (Writer's Digest Books) is somewhat better written. An excellent marketing companion to both is John Kremer's extremely detailed *1001 Ways to Market Your Books* (Open Horizons).

Should you even consider self-publishing? Let me share a quick checklist beginning on page 141, that will give you one way of seeing whether this alternative publishing path is worth further consideration or you should seek the less risky, less profitable and much slower, but far more common, path of putting your publishing future in the hands of the regular publishing houses.

Publishing your own nonfiction niche marketed book

Niche publishing is the brightest and most profitable light in the publishing world for freelancers. The major difference between it and standard self-publishing is that a niche publisher almost never sells to bookstores or libraries; rather it sells directly to buyers in its niche, usually by mail (often 90 percent or more).

Niche published books are need-meeting or hope-fulfilling for preselected, specific buyers, for example, *The Chocolate Lover's Worldwide Catalog* (for lovers of chocolate), *Closing Techniques of America's Ten Best Car Salesfolk* (for car salesfolk) or *Standard Operating Procedures for Pediatric Dentists* (you guessed it).

Until recently, books for universes smaller than many thousand were outlandishly expensive to print, without considering hot or cold type, rubber cement, cut-and-paste assembly, rubylith covers and months of waiting in line until one of the few book printers got around to producing your masterpiece.

Then came the computer. Now, any writer with publishing aspirations can produce a tightly targeted book that is page-made at home, zip it off to the printer for a short turnaround, then sell it to several hundred, or many thousand, eager souls at costs half of what they were a decade ago.

The hardest part, and the heart, of niche publishing is finding a

The 18 Key Steps to Self-Publishing

1. Find a subject that others will pay to know (more) about. Nothing is more important, unless you plan to give your book away after having spent from $3,500 to $8,000 or more to have it printed. Ask yourself *why* they would pay to read what you wrote. What will it do for them? Make them richer? Prettier? Happier? Sexier? Save their marriages? Reduce car repair costs? Help them find new jobs? Unless the readers will receive obvious and believable rewards from reading your opus, get somebody else to publish it, reduce the material to an article (or articles) or sell the information some other way.

2. Figure out the other ways your potential book buyers can find out what you would tell them in your book. If other books or pamphlets are readily available, particularly at a cost far below what you can match, why would they pay more for your book? (There are reasons: better packaging, brighter writing, etc., but the odds are against you. Better to change the topic slightly, approach it from a different—and more appealing—angle.)

3. Determine how you would sell your masterpiece: bookstores, mail order, county fair booths, swap meets, the Internet, seminars, etc. Then look more closely at those selling outlets to see if anybody else is making money selling similar (or any) books that way. Particularly study the appearance, price, length and topic angle of the books you must compete against.

4. Don't write yet!

5. Estimate the length of your book (the page total must be divisible by four, better if by sixteen), read the Poynter or Ross chapter about printing, draw up a sample "request for quotation" and send it (fax is far faster) to no less than six regular book printers. Keep reading the Poynter or Ross book until you get the quotations back.

6. Study the quotations (or bids) closely. Mentally add 10 percent to the total for tax (which you needn't pay to the printer if you get a state resale tax number) and other hidden items, or inflation that may appear before the books arrive in printed form. If you plan to advertise, the amount of the best bid will probably

be about half of the total expenditures you will have to prepare and sell your books—if they sell.

7. This is the time to decide whether you want to risk your money by self-publishing, so selling must now be addressed. List all of the ways you will make your book available to potential buyers. Kremer's book is particularly valuable here. Estimate the number of purchases each might bring, then the costs of securing those sales: discounts, fulfillment, mailing, credit card costs, bad debts (figure 1 percent of your sale income), shipping and storage damages. Then calculate the means and costs of promotion, including flyers, mailing, copies for reviewers and influencers, phone, etc. Is the potential income significantly higher than the expenses, and do you have the money to tide you over in the meantime? If the books sell and you keep the costs down, self-publishing can be extremely profitable—but almost always in the long run. In the short run, your money will be tied up in paper in your bedroom or garage. It's a gamble. Self-publishing only makes sense if you have a salable topic, the book is well packaged, you keep production costs low (while turning out a marketable item) and you care enough about the business/promotion side to work as hard at selling the book as you do at writing it.

8. You still want to self-publish? Great!

9. Now write a book that is so direct, clear, vital, comprehensive, needed and valuable that anybody would be a fool not to buy it. Also, a book you won't be ashamed to show to your friends.

10. If you write well, a major problem is finding others who will read it and offer honest criticism, plus no-nonsense proofreading. Then having the humility and self-assurance to make changes where necessary.

11. If you don't write well, you can pay somebody else to write the book for you (which may cost from $4,000 to $10,000) or you can write the best book possible, then pay a professional far less to rewrite it in final form. In either case you will need still another, unrelated person to give it a thorough proofing, preferably at the final-draft stage before the manuscript is typed in book form, then again after it is typed but before printing.

12. In the meantime, the promotional steps that all three books suggest must be interwoven at the appropriate times as the book is being assembled. Particularly important are the galley proofs you may want to send to library reviewers.

13. A few additional "tips" or clarifications might help from here on, presuming you are letting Poynter or Ross (plus Kremer) guide you through the steps of putting a book together and selling it. One, do as much of the work yourself as possible, paying key professionals to assist where their labors are critical to the book's appearance or cost. Think of yourself as a general contractor who hires out for the specialty work, in this case, the cover design and all artwork, proofing and printing. Why add employees? Why pay for pasting up pages when you can use pagemaking in your computer software? Why rush through your book—if it takes three days longer, the book will come out three days later.

14. Concerning your cover and internal artwork, your best investment, unless you are experienced in this area, is to hire a professional graphics person to design and lay out the cover and assist with the general design and artwork contents of the text, including type fonts and margins, headers and footers. Get bids for this. Tell designers what you want to do, show them some of the text, give them as much information as they need to know to do their job well and ask them for a time and cost figure in writing. Review closely the work they have done for others. Packaging is crucial to selling your book, particularly a cover if it's a bookstore or library seller. People *do* buy books by their covers! More important, distributors simply won't handle books that don't look professional.

15. Most books today are either produced in camera-ready form on at least a 300 dpi (better, 600 dpi) laser printer and sent to the book printer in directly copiable form (with spaces for artwork inserts, the artwork and clear instructions), or on computer disk according to the printer's specific instructions, with artwork and instructions also sent. Work closely with the printer you select for final printing. (The cover artwork is usually submitted at the same time, with separations having been made by the cover artist in consultation with the printer.)

16. Sell your book as if it were gilded. Tell everybody about it. Be miserly with free copies—do you hand out dollar bills to anybody who asks? Give them to your family, a friend or two, all involved in its preparation. Others: If you'd fix their toilets free, give them free copies! Everybody else pays—unless giving away one copy will sell three more, as with reviewers, wholesalers or teachers who might seriously consider it for use in their classes.

17. Miss no opportunity to sell yourself as its author, in person, on radio or TV, to groups. Bring some copies to sell, where appropriate. If you have something to say and it makes sense, so must your book. The ultimate success of your book is most influenced by your belief in it. If you don't believe in it, either don't write it or write it and let somebody else sell it. If you do believe in it and it makes economic sense to self-publish, let everyone know it's available and why they should buy it!

18. Making your own book a "best-seller"—that is a book that sells out its printing—takes a lot of work, endless hustle and guts. It's also easier if you order a small volume of books (no more than 1,500 to 2,000) at the outset, then have more printed as it takes off. There are few satisfactions in the world like helping others through your words that you put in print and in their hands.

market you want to mingle with for the next few years, then identifying a critical need that market must solve and ardently wants to. Your book is that market's solution and you, its author, an expert on how to meet the market's need.

The second hardest part of niche publishing is the back-to-front process of market-certifying your idea before writing a word. This procedure is completely foreign to those used to working with the larger publishing houses or selling to traditional markets through distributors and bookstores.

That process can be summed up in three letters, TCE, which stand for targeting, customizing and expanding.

Targeting is the first step: Select the target market and the topic, then check the *SRDS Direct Mail List Rates & Data* to see (1) if those in the market are accessible by current, affordable mailing lists and (2) if there are enough of them to turn a profit at what you must charge for the book.

Guesswork isn't good enough, because selling by mail is so expensive. A test is prudent. For about $150 the potential publisher can see if she should risk (and hopefully reap) many thousands of dollars more. The test is built around a comprehensive one-page flyer that explains what the book is about, a table of contents, a bio about the author and a list of the promises the book will keep, plus the form of cover and binding, approximate number of pages and cost. (To test two or three different prices, you divide the mailing into subdivisions and change the book cost on each subdivision.)

That flyer is sent to several hundred people randomly chosen from your market. With the flyer is a short letter asking the recipient's help in completing and returning a two-question postcard, which is also included. This preaddressed, stamped postcard asks

☐ yes ☐ no   I would buy a book
              titled "_____"

☐ yes ☐ no   I would pay $ _____ for it.

Comments:

A quick calculation of the returning postcards (most will arrive within fifteen days) will tell you if the book's publication is worth your gamble and effort. Here's a gauge that might help you: A book selling for $30, half of which is profit, bought by 10 percent of your universe of 33,500 people will earn you $50,250 profit. (It will probably cost you about $43,000 to gross $93,250.)

If the book's a go, then "C" (customize) it. Write it specifically to your niche audience: their needs, interests and vocabulary. Is your market 65 percent female, median age forty-four? Then most of the photos and interviews will focus on women in their forties. Do they buy only cloth books? Expect to pay $35 and up? Want lots of graphs and charts? Don't let them down!

The beauty of niched books is that they are bought directly from you, which means you have buyers' names, addresses and probably phone numbers. That database is a gold mine. With it you can let those customers know about more good books or products in their field of interest—most of which you'll buy at discount from others at the outset to resell, until you expand your own production to meet the needs.

Niche self-publishing can be the root of your own empire-building by writing and speaking. That usually starts with the right niched book excellently produced and well marketed.

That's where the "E" (expanding) fits in. If you are meeting a vital need and the buyers acknowledge your expertise, they will look to you to help them in other ways and/or by other means. Some will choose additional books (about related topics, case studies, updates). Others will want the same or similar information through a seminar or speech, on audio- or videotape, computerized on disk, as a report or newsletter or in articles. Hence the empire.

Three books are critical here. All by Gordon Burgett (yes, me), the keynote text is *Publishing to Niche Markets*, which gives chapters of detail on all items mentioned above. The core book about empire-building (with niche publishing as the most profitable means of displaying one's expertise) is, properly, *Empire-Building by Writing and Speaking*. And to extend the selling beyond the publishing core, *Niche Marketing for Writers, Speakers, and Entrepreneurs*.

You want to write and sell a book? If it's nonfiction (as most are), you have three choices of publishers: one is the standard publishers you usually associate with bookstore or library books, and the other two are you, following one of two different marketing strategies. If it's fiction, find the major houses that publish similar fiction.

CHAPTER EIGHT

Newspaper Selling With a Cover Letter

Selling to newspapers is a dance to another tune.

Life at a newspaper resounds to a much faster beat than at magazines, and infinitely faster than for book publishers. Fifty pages of copy, or more, are published every day, sometimes in two or three versions in the same twenty-four-hour period. Newspaper editors have deadlines that are notoriously inelastic—and readers about as intransigent if, in the scramble to get the copy into print, you inject inaccuracies. So speed and accuracy are the coins of trade there.

Which means that selling to newspapers differs considerably from magazine selling. The luxury of deliberate, courtly query letters and leisurely fashioned replies, with the copy wending its way in weeks or even months later, is highly unlikely. Copy is sent in complete and, ideally, is so well constructed and tightly woven that all the editor must do is read it once and insert it for inclusion.

Theoretically, you can hope to sell to a newspaper anything that leaps off the page and cries to appear before local eyes. In reality, this means whatever the editor likes but the staff isn't writing, or can't be bought as good (or at least as cheaply) from the syndicates to which the newspaper subscribes. Then it might be bought from you if (1) there's sufficient cash in the editor's budget, (2) the editor knows your copy exists and (3) there is space left after the ads, required fillers and news items have been locked in.

There are two problems with selling copy to newspapers. One, they work independently, so you must sell to each of the several hundred that buy (eagerly or out of desperation) from freelancers. Two, they would far prefer to receive the finished manuscripts than query letters, which means you must actually write the words in final form before you know whether they want to read and buy it. A third problem, usually, is their low rate of pay.

Keep in mind, too, that writing for newspapers across the land requires a key modification: Directions or geographic references must be equally applicable to all readers. If you are writing from Iowa about Montana and suggest that to get there you should drive west, the Oregon readers, blithely following your instructions, have a very hard, wet drive ahead!

Newspaper markets for freelancers

The travel section by far buys the most freelance copy. The main article (generally 2,000–4,000 words long, with color slides) is probably written by the travel editor (or a travel editor from another newspaper), but sometimes you can muscle into the top slot. Your best bet is with a "second," one of the two to four smaller articles in the travel section, often 800–1,700 words—I've found that 1,200–1,350 works the best. Black-and-white photos accompany most seconds; some carry no photos at all. Odd, offbeat locales; a low-budget slant to accompany a longer, upscale destination piece; an update on a popular destination, short and specific—those work particularly well for seconds. The pay? From $50 to $450, but most are between $100 and $200, plus photos.

Food editors are fairly receptive to appropriate pieces, particularly for holidays. Humor works in this section too, as long as the primary focus is on the food or process. Sometimes the lifestyle, business and consumer editors will also nibble on sharp copy. Straight news is the hardest to sell, unless you have the inside path to people or facts that cry for front-page revelation. The pay varies. Think of $100 to $200.

One well-trod path to a newspaper byline (and modest check) is the "op-ed" (opposite the editorial page) section. Here the passwords are short and tight: 400–800 words, sometimes a bit longer. Anything goes as long as it adds punch and insight: humor, wit, satire, a clever twist, the opposite view. From $50 to $150 per sale is common.

As you can see, if you worked just one newspaper from the outside, you'd starve to death in short order. Even the insiders barely make it on the chronically low writing wages. So your best bet is to write crisp, compelling copy and sell it, without a whit of change, to many newspapers simultaneously. In other words, you can write one article, make many copies of the same text (word-for-word, without customization) and send it simultaneously to many editors.

Often if one buys it, several will. Instead of a typical $150 newspaper travel sale for 1,300 well-chosen words, you easily earn $500 or more for the same prose, plus multiple photo sales, which might add $150 to $200 more. The additional cost to you? A few more bucks to copy, some stamps and additional mailing time.

If you had to sell to each editor separately, and if altogether different, final copy had to be sent to each just to be considered, the time and energy needed wouldn't be worth the pursuit. But *simultaneous submissions* puts newspaper sales back in the ball game!

Alas, as with all good things, there are some stipulations: (1) those to whom you submit must be editors of regional newspapers and (2) they must be located at least one hundred miles from each other.

The reason for the first and second are the same: The buying editor doesn't want readers to have seen the copy in print in another publication before or about the same time they read it on that editor's pages.

There are four national newspapers. The rest are regional. The four are *The New York Times, The Wall Street Journal, USA Today* and *The Christian Science Monitor.* If you appear on their pages you cannot help but overlap on the local readership somewhere.

Not selling to them will not be fatal. *The New York Times* pays well but it seldom buys from us, *The Wall Street Journal* seeks the appropriate business slant and thus requires special writing anyway, *USA Today* buys almost nothing from the public and *The Christian Science Monitor* does but pays far too little to use up the opportunity to sell the same material simultaneously and often.

The 100-mile rule prevents you from entering war circles, where the editors read each other's copy regularly, in part to protect their own turfs. So you can't send and sell the same masterpiece to both the *Chicago Tribune* and the *Chicago Sun Times* or to the key Los

Angeles and Long Beach newspapers or *The Washington Post* and the *Baltimore Sun*. But you could send it to one of the two in each example, and if refused, then send it to the other. (I'd resist telling the second editor, however, that the first refused it!)

Thus, you could send the same exact manuscript to a dozen (or forty or ninety) travel editors of regional newspapers that were out of each other's 100-mile circles, and if five, fifteen or thirty of them bought it, you're way ahead of the game. Almost all editors buy travel, or other freelance newspaper articles, for one-time use in their circulation or distribution areas, which means about one hundred miles out. (Some will ask for greater use but will be satisfied as long as they know you neither sell the copy nationally nor to a nearby competitor.)

What you are doing is mini-syndicating your work. Hat's off to you for being that industrious. So if the editor asks if he can buy it for syndication, you must say no since there is no way to prevent it being sold to those publications you are already soliciting. (Syndicated sales often pay no more, and when they do it is a pittance, so there is far less lost to you than potentially gained through your own, other sales. Will it hurt future sales? I've been asked if an article of mine could be used to syndication several dozen times by different editors. I've kindly declined, and it's yet to lose me a sale.)

(Let's discuss Internet issues in chaper ten for both newspaper and magazine sales.)

As for writing first, then submitting the finished manuscript with a cover note, the hassle is (1) the preparation and mailing and (2) trying to find a style and slant acceptable to a wide swath of editors.

There's no way around the paper shuffle other than to use a system that works well for all, sticking to it and getting the submissions out often.

Newspaper weekly supplements
Much of what was said about the travel articles applies here. The same choice of national or regional markets, 100-mile circle and ability to submit simultaneously.

Yet these are run more like a magazine within a newspaper. *Parade* and *Family Weekly* are examples at the national level, inserted into the regular newspaper, almost always on Sunday.

Most newspapers have their own weeklies full of features, some articles national in scope but somehow relevant locally, usually with a local slant or setting.

You usually have an option here of querying as described in the magazine section of this book or submitting prepared copy, done in the manner described in the next pages but directed to the specific editor and emphasizing the local tie-in, if possible.

Let me offer two examples that sold well for me.

My widest newspaper seller (about twenty-five sales—I was lax on keeping copies or records at the outset. I hadn't read my book yet!) was a humor piece about "Fifteen-Year Reunions," a spoof on latter-day class gatherings that was set in a generic location that could be Anywhere, U.S.A. Even the "Fifteen-Year" element was odd: Most gather at decade markers—tenth, twentieth, etc. So in my cover note I simply asked if any of the readers of _____ had ever attended a class reunion? I listed three or four funny, stressful, bewildering things that are common to such meetings. Then I asked if the readers might not identify with the article enclosed.

Their curiosity piqued, many editors found the fun appropriate to their readers, and at an average of $300 apiece, I in turn found their recompense particularly pleasing.

The second example was based on a generic article, a look at the year 1876 during the bicentennial of 1976. It was a whimsical, humorous look at where America was "100 years ago" that touched many topics of general interest—the shooting of Bill Hickok, the start of major league baseball, the magnificent Philadelphia Exposition, the visit of the kings of both Brazil and the Sandwich Islands, "Custer's Last Stand," the invention of linoleum, the publishing of *Robert's Rules of Order* and so on. To that I promised to insert specific sections appropriate to their cities (three editors bit on that). It sold fourteen times in various newspaper renditions and earned from $320 to $600 per sale.

Why these sold widely is that any reader anywhere found in them something she wants to know more about or could laugh at and with.

The topic range of the newspaper weeklies is extremely wide, so travel, food and other section items bought from freelancers sometimes work here too.

The only submission difference, when using a cover letter, is that it can be a full page, rather than the half-page note generally used. Instead of stapling it to the front of the newspaper article, the cover letter is unattached and is sent in front of the article, which is paper clipped, not stapled. Consider the newspaper weekly supplements to be like magazines that are simply sold to as if they were newspapers.

Cover letter guidelines

The actual manuscript is no different than that sent to magazine editors (as described in chapter six). What differs is the cover letter that accompanies it, stapled in front of the manuscript at the upper left corner and covering no more than the top half so that the only thing covered is the title, the byline and the number of words included in the text.

Incidentally, it's not necessary to indicate on the manuscript that it is offered for simultaneous submission or to which newspapers it is being sent. The editor will assume (or will ask if concerned) that you are following the "rules" explained: that it is not being sent to a nationally circulated newspaper (or magazine) nor to any other within one hundred miles. That you're sending it out simultaneously is understood: How else could you afford to work this venue?

Assuming then that the copy is properly universalized, what personalizes it is the cover letter (which, at a half page, is more properly a cover note).

A typical cover note, in this case about a possible trip to Paraguay, might read like the one on page 153.

Let's quickly review the elements of this cover note and why they appear as and where they do.

First, the editor would far rather read my synopsis stapled to the front of the manuscript than have to read the entire article. Time is the issue—plus the likelihood that in a few paragraphs the editor can tell whether my writing is worth further consideration.

The first sentence gets right to it: What is this article about? Paraguay. Why would the readers care? The dictator is gone (after 182 straight years, which I should have mentioned), the airfare is a real bargain, so is the room and board, and you can still continue on to Rio or Buenos Aires nearby and make a real trip of it.

I just got back; it won't be an encyclopedic piece written for a Latin

Gordon Burgett
(Address)
(City, State ZIP)
(Phone/Fax)

Dear Travel Editor:

Visiting Paraguay is the thing to do since Stroessner's exit, Air Paraguay began bargain fares and low hotel and food prices make it the jumping off spot for Rio de Janeiro or Buenos Aires. I just returned from two weeks of seeing what this landlocked haven of cattle and wood has to offer the eager American. What's worth doing is spectacular; the rest is best traded for more days in Brazil. The article tells all! (The article is also available on disk, which I can mail or send by modem.)

I'll gladly send an assortment of 16 b/w's to choose from, if interested. And I have scores of excellent slides, particularly of the mission ruins and the waterfalls, you can select from. Just let me know. About me? Some 1,600 articles in print; author of *The Travel Writer's Guide*. You needn't return the manuscript, just your verdict in the enclosed SASE. Hope we can share these insights and advice with you antsy readers, particularly before they head south to escape our winter.

(My signature)

American history or studies class. Direct observation, current and factual, gathered during a two-week stay. I'm an American so I likely see with eyes similar to the readers'. A landlocked haven of cattle and wood. (Every word must work when you have just room for 180 of them.)

"What's worth doing is spectacular; the rest is best traded for more days in Brazil." Interesting, thinks the editor. What's so spectacular? Why Brazil? And this Burgett isn't trying to tell me Paraguay is unbridled paradise, which would mean superlatives outdueling each other to justify his writing about it or to pay back, with a mention, the hotels and restaurants where he was comped!

He can send the text by disk or modem. Great. We won't have to enter it again.

A wide choice of photos, in black and white or color. Ruins and waterfalls.

And the guy's been in print, even wrote a book about travel writing, so he's less a gamble. He puts it on the line: Just read the copy, he says, and if it's what you want, tell him if you want the photography to review.

The time is now, he says, before the gringos head south to escape the winter. They're going to Paraguay to escape the winter? Well, a bit overblown but why not?

Standard format

At the top is a return address (with my name, in case the editor can't read my handwritten signature on the bottom). Included is my phone number should the editor wish to call when considering the article or adapting it to print. (It's not uncommon—it happens to me perhaps 20 percent of the time—for a newspaper travel editor to call to check out specific items mentioned or ask for additional information as the article is being slightly rewritten, trimmed to fit or added to from other related copy to expand the text.)

Once you have established a corps of editors who are particularly receptive to your submissions, you'll address cover notes specifically to them. In the beginning, however, you can address "Dear Travel Editor:" and keep your note sufficiently broad to cover all.

The first paragraph in the cover note must sell the article attached, for one simple reason: Most editors won't read a word of the text unless drawn in by the note. If the first paragraph of the note doesn't make the article sound so exciting, so needed for that editor's pages (and success), he won't read beyond it. How do I know? Travel editors tell me so!

Capture the key elements in sharp prose. Tell why every reader could scarcely resist your message and why an editor would be a fool to pass it up. But do it in context, in the style of the piece you have attached.

The second paragraph probably tells of the availability of photos, their usability (at least call them good to excellent, if that's the case; if not, why are you offering them?), and that you'll gladly send some proofs (sixteen works for me) for review, "or pick out the five best."

If you have no photos, continue highlighting key elements that sell the text. Presume the editor can get photos or won't be interested. Don't provide weepy explanations about the broken shutter or how the camera was eaten by a creature that is nameless in English!

If the key selling element is the photography, with the text to pull that together, reverse the paragraph order. If you have a face-on, full-detail shot of the Abominable Snowman or, less likely, an ugly grandchild, explain that in paragraph one, then how the article attached is the explanatory text, in paragraph two.

Paragraph three is the closer, with instructions so the editor knows how you want to receive your good news.

Don't forget to include a SASE large enough to get the cover note back (with instructions handwritten on the back) or a postcard, which might appear like the example below, with your return address and stamp (or indicia) on the back.

Make as many copies of the manuscript as you wish to mail, write

---

Submission Title: _____

_____ Yep, am holding for possible future use.
_____ Let's see your b/w photos.
_____ Let's see your color slides.
_____ Could you send a sidebar about _____
_____ Not this time!

Comments:

Name _____
Publication _____

a cover note, make the same number of copies, attach one to each, prepare an SASE or return postcard and send off the submissions. All that's left is the check cashing!

Subject, style and slant for newspapers

As for finding a subject, style and slant most editors might buy, that comes in part from reading what is widely used and staying close to it. By studying what editors buy and precisely how it is written.

What do you write about for newspaper editors? Anything that will interest their readers. No print vehicle is as hungry for copy or as wide ranging in the kinds of things it covers. While its focus is on the present—*new* is the key part of *newspaper*—that encompasses all things that lead up to the present as well as where we are headed in the future.

What would few editors buy? Hate pieces: "I hate (this site)," "Travel stinks," "All cook books are rip-offs." Look at the ads surrounding the section copy and ask how many would be there if the editor slammed the key topic more than very, very rarely? How long would the editor be there? There are other restrictions. Foul language seldom appears in family print. Particular newspapers have political biases.

But most vary little from the average person's understanding of life as we live it, now and in the area where it prints. It is hard to think of much, if subjectively written, directed at the reader, and framed to expand their understanding or knowledge, that couldn't find its way onto some page somewhere. So finding salable topics is less your problem than putting them before the right editor's eyes in a way that makes them appealing.

A couple of years back I stumbled on a no-brainer that was picked up widely, mostly as a main article (2,700 words, plenty of color slides, at an average of about $450 a sale) but also for seconds as well. It's a good example of what has the best chance of selling, as a major or second article to almost any editor.

It was the topic of the cover note you just read: Paraguay, the landlocked, half-mysterious South American country plagued by centuries of the most ruthless dictators in the hemisphere. Most of the people speak Guaraní, Nazis were rumored to have sought refuge their en masse under General Stroessner's rule, wood and yerba maté were the major import and the movie *The Mission* was supposedly shot at the seventeenth-century Jesuit ruins said to be widely found and remarkably intact throughout the country. Enough curiosity piques for half a dozen articles.

Then Stroessner was thrown out, the military vowed to return the nation to democracy, the borders were opened to outsiders and Air Paraguay had a low-priced round-trip special from Miami (with a free Rio add-on). How could I resist? The question and theme? What was Paraguay like for the visiting American tourist?

It's always a gamble, of course, trying to second-guess what travel editors want. But it was easy in that case. I used the "I" rule. If I find the topic irresistible and I suspect that others would too, I write about it—and enough editors buy it. Like Paraguay.

So I went, spent several weeks finding the subjects that were the most exciting or different and about which information shared would be new (which is what newspapers seek), gathered all I could about each, took photos while I visited the sites, interviewed, recorded impressions and brought it all together when I returned. Then I wrote the master manuscripts, determined an order of submission, made enough copies to mail to the chosen editors and waited for the acceptances (and checks), requests for photo prints or slides (for acceptances) or rejections. If rejected, I then sent a copy of that same manuscript (with a new cover note) to another travel editor of a publication in that same 100-mile circle, if one existed.

An important aside. Since Paraguay is an expensive poke from California and two weeks visiting anywhere can be costly, I probably wouldn't have made this trip without querying magazines for articles and receiving some go-aheads well in advance to add to the income from the newspaper article sales. But nearby pieces or a few hundred miles to explore a solid newspaper topic would be well within my risk range!

What did the newspapers find sufficiently irresistible to buy? Most wanted the major, 2,700-word article about the country in general and whether it was worth seeing, the conditions and plenty of travel details. Others wanted seconds about Asunción, the missions along the country's southern border with Argentina and the breathtaking Fôz de

Iguaçú, the waterfalls near the country's second largest city, Ciudad del Este, but actually lying between Brazil and Argentina where the three nations touch.

Finding newspaper addresses

Names of editors and newspaper locations must be sought in other sources than those for magazines.

A complete list of newspapers, with staff, is found in the *Working Press of the Nation*. At any one time only about 75 to 80 percent of the editors are buying travel, and the percentage of editors buying in other sections, while guesswork at any time, is probably closer to 50 percent. Even worse, those who are buying continually change as budgets disappear, their stock gets glutted with usable copy or the syndicates temporarily meet their needs.

One shortcut to creating your own list of travel editors is to buy "100 Best U.S. Newspaper Travel Markets," an annually updated (January 1) list of editors who buy travel, in Avery-label address format on paper or on computer disk (indicate which and, if disk, whether you use a Macintosh or IBM/compatible). With shipping, it costs $11.50. Contact Communication Unlimited, P.O. Box 6405, Santa Maria, CA 93456, or (805) 937-8711, fax (805) 937-3035.

The best list, over time, is of those editors who find your copy interesting, thorough, accurate, honest and widely researched. A cadre of reliable buyers eager to read your newest submission is what, in the long run, makes newspaper writing fun and profitable.

CHAPTER NINE

Writing and Submitting Your Articles

W hile this book is selling oriented, it would be foolish not to at least highlight the key points you should know about writing articles that sell. Other books will walk you through the details in greater depth, if you need further help. Let's focus here on the bare bones of composing copy that sells.

If you have a target magazine in mind, nothing is more important than a detailed study of previous issues of that magazine before you send copy to its editor. Use the tool called "How to Study a Printed Magazine Article," in chapter two, to determine precisely what that editor buys—and, by extension, what you must produce to get on those pages. Find the last three issues, pick out at least one article from each that is closest to what you have in mind (by subject, tone, length and/ or style) and pull those words apart to see why the writer put them together that way.

Remember, that way was good enough to have been bought by the editor. What better way to figure out what the editor buys than to read what was just bought? "That sucks out all my creativity!" you shout. Hardly. It shows you the box—that boundary within which the editor buys, in terms of content and sytle—within which you can be as creative as your juices allow.

Is the editor seeking four-letter expletives, graphic confrontation and exclamations at the end of each phrase or sentence? Go to it. Or does the editor want parlor room English, all people's names preceded by their titles, precise dollar amounts (including cents) and each paragraph exactly three sentences long? Every publication has its peculiarities, its dos and don'ts. The dos are inside the box, the don'ts aren't. If you include the don'ts in your copy, you won't be on those pages.

This is also the time and way to study the ratio, quantity and type of facts, quotes and anecdotes used, plus to judge the amount and level of humor employed.

If the publication is fact driven—lists, columns, charts, details— your copy must include the same kind and depth of facts.

If your study article from each of the last three issues includes quotes from four different people, guess what? You need at least three but probably no more than five different people quoted in your article. Four is best. (No MENSA membership required here.) And if they are all employees of the company being discussed or all rangers at the park or police on the beat, is a message being sent about who you should interview? Are the interviews long, detailed and aggressive in tone? Are they short and humorous? Another message?

Study the anecdotes. Are they historical—the recounting of Dom Pedro II's visit to Philadelphia in 1876, how a gold hunter got lost in the Klondike (in his own words), why a certain street got its name? Are they first-person, I-did-this accounts? Are they all third person? Is the article simply a string of accounts, or are there no anecdotes at all? That tells you how amenable the editor is to anecdotal content.

In short, most articles are a blend of those three elements. Certain topics lend themselves to a certain ratio. Editors tend to favor a certain combination, sometimes formatted in a certain order. Increase the chances of your copy being bought by discovering that bias, then writing that way.

There is a critical fourth element to that bias: humor. Some topics don't lend themselves to it. Some editors wouldn't know, or use, humor if they sat on whoopee cushions with their shoes on fire. So suggesting mirthful text in funny query letters to them has as much chance of being bought as would a manuscript sent in jocular Sanskrit.

If you are comfortable with humor, can sprinkle it to the same degree throughout the text and both the topic lends itself to it and the editor uses it, including it will increase your salability considerably, because most editors do want it and so few writers can make it work. But study first to see if it's welcome, how it is used if it is and if it will not impede you realizing the purpose of the article. Then remember to write the query letter in the same humorous tone as the article to follow, while also doing all the things a query must do.

Nobody has devised a formula or means for how to write creatively any more than someone can teach you how to think. At most, others can share what seems to work best to create articles that will more likely be used by editors in their publications. A critical component of writing falls outside the boundaries of direction. The art of writing is finding the precise words, tone, combination and style that lift what is being said above the mechanical means of saying it. It is that ill-defined and unteachable something that converts simple words into magic.

Do not, however, equate unbridled art with selling articles. Article "art" must do more than glow—it must inform, instruct and explain. Editors do not abandon their publications' purposes simply to display writers' inner yearnings, revelations or onomatopoeic bleatings—unless those are the kinds of publications they edit. But all editors want art (or creativity) as a valuable component to make their articles excel and the messages shine.

Two things can be taught or at least explained: the structure and the mechanics of an article.

The structure of articles that sell

Nine elements must be accounted for in any article you wish to sell: the purpose, the lead, the transitional paragraph, word flow and transitions between paragraphs, word choice and paragraph length, the conclusion and the title.

The purpose

The purpose is less a component than a reason and a direction that can also be used as a measuring tool. It is why the article is being written and why the editor will buy it. If the purpose of an article is to explain how to prune an apricot tree but instead it explains how to rid one's yard of moles, the author has dug a fatal hole in prose: That article is DOA. The editor bought apricot pruning in the query letter and got mole murder instead. Failure to deliver an article achieving the approved purpose, however clever or amusing are the words that arrive, will get a sad nod from the editor, perhaps an angry rejection letter and certain inclusion on the editor's list of those from whom he will not buy in the future.

There is a straightforward technique that should help you define your article's purpose.

First write down the key words of that topic. Then ask what benefits one would receive by reading an article about that topic—or what needs would be met. (They are two sides of the same coin: Needs met are benefits realized.) Which of those needs or benefits are most central to the purpose of the magazine in which you want the article to appear?

From those answers decide, in one sentence, the purpose of your article. Write it out. If you can't define that purpose in one sentence, stop. You don't know what you're writing about yet. Work harder on the definition until the sentence is clear and singular. That is the purpose statement.

Then convert that sentence into a question. That is your working question. Everything in your article answers that question. If something doesn't, save it for another article.

To answer that question, you usually need to answer secondary questions. These are almost always defined by the "5 *w*'s and *h*" of journalism: who, what, why, where, when and how. Write out every secondary question that comes to mind. Combine or restate them where they overlap. Then put them in some logical order. That provides a rough outline for the writing of your article.

It also provides an evaluative tool to see whether the purpose was achieved by the final article and whether the key, or all, questions were answered in getting there.

The lead

A lead is like dressing for an interview: If what you wear turns the interviewer off, it's virtually impossible to get the job however well you speak or what you say. The lead is the article's clothes. After the title, it's the first thing the reader sees. Its job is to grab that reader's interest and make him want to read more.

The first paragraph containing the lead is what sells both the editor and the reader. It gets their attention and whets their appetites. Many call it the "hook" because it "hooks" or "draws in" the reader. If you doubt this, read the leads of the articles in the publications you want to sell to. Chances are, they open with a compelling setting, a quick act of heroism, a vivid example, a sharp quote, some offbeat fact or a patch of humor. They set the pace, inject the spirit, capture curiosity and provide the pull that makes the reader want to continue. Study what is being used, then stick close to it in length and style. Keep your leads short, a sentence or two.

You needn't write a lead first. Just start writing the story and worry about the lead later. Once you know where the piece is going, try to come up with several leads, either as you're writing the body of the text or after it's completed. Then select the best of the lot and bring the rest of the piece into line. Usually a few verb changes and some new transitions are all it takes.

But don't write a lead in ten seconds then spend ten hours trying to fit the rest of the words into its promise. Think of the lead as the most malleable element of the article. It can be changed again and again, at any stage.

Finally, leads by their nature often highlight a more exotic shard of fact or action from a larger, less exotic body, to grab attention. Yet that shard can't be so remote from the theme that you've lured the readers in only to have to complete the article with something else entirely.

For example, let's say you are writing about the vagaries of the English language and you state in your lead, "Less than one tenth of 1 percent of those speaking English as their native tongue know the only adjective in the language that is spelled differently for males and females. Imagine how confused newcomers to English must be just with to, too and two."

If it's true, that's a perfectly fine lead because you can write for pages about the other oddities without the reader feeling you tricked him in under false premises. (Incidentally, I have no idea about the percentage but that adjective is *blond/blonde*.)

Yet if you start your article, "Men who eat cabbage twice daily for ten years will live an average of 112 years," then you segue into thirty-six paragraphs about the secrets of growing cabbage successfully, you're going to have one irked editor and thousands of bewildered, then angry, cabbage-eating readers.

The point: Get the reader's attention with the truth, then keep it with related truths about the same thing.

The transitional (or organizational) paragraph

This crucial and seldom discussed element is hard to describe. It follows the lead and usually tells where the article is going and how it will get there. But sometimes it's not needed at all.

Since leads often distort the direction of a piece by focusing on a more spectacular or bizarre aspect of the subject, it is then left to the second (and sometimes third and even fourth) paragraph to straighten out the theme, set up the process of discussing it and establish the true tone. That is particularly true when the lead is humorous or contains wordplay.

For example, the lead and transition paragraph might be

"The stage presentation of *Evita* was a 100 percent, no-doubt-about-it pineapple in São Paulo."

"In the U.S. it would have been a bomb, a clunker, a dud or—to keep it in the realm of fruit—a lemon. But anything that truly fails in Brazil is an *abacaxi*, or pineapple. When they sought the most descriptive slang in Portuguese, they didn't come to English for models."

The article will then give more illustrations. "In the comic books, when our hero lands a solid right on some villain's chin, the text reads POW! He gets off easy in Brazil: POOF!"

The transitional paragraph most often tells what the article is really about and how it will be discussed. We know in the example that the rest of the article will show how different the words are between English and Portuguese to express the same concepts—and that it will be done with humor.

Often the transitional paragraph shows that the topic will be presented chronologically, by city, by steps of development, etc. It is also called the "bridge" because it links the lead to the body by explaining how the first will be explained in the second. Without a well-designed transitional paragraph, many, perhaps most, articles would make little sense. So study them closely. They can be the difference between selling success and a lot of words going nowhere.

Word flow and transitions between paragraphs

Once the article is progressing logically to its conclusion, your job is to keep your readers on track, moving smoothly from the first paragraph to the next. That is done by word choice and smooth transitioning from one idea, emotion, example or point to the next so the progression is fully comprehensible, enjoyable and seamless.

Your article's organization and its revelation to the reader in either the transitional paragraph(s) or soon after are the most useful tools here. If you tell them there are four ways to control depression or that mountain ash trees (which need mates nearby to propagate) are usually planted in one of six patterns, it is easy from then on to logically move from the first example to the second to the third. At times you will remind the reader that "this is the fourth of the six most common planting patterns" so they recall what the numbers refer to.

Linking is also done from one paragraph to another, to keep the idea and words flowing in a sensible, easy-to-follow progression. If you're explaining how three visiting Brazilian students overcame their *saudade* (loneliness) when visiting the U.S., you might speak about Maria Lourdes's particular experiences with it for one segment. The first paragraph of the segment devoted to João, the second student, then, might begin,

> While Maria Lourdes was volunteering at the hospital, João was the first person on the field the day that soccer practice began.

Later, when it's Pedro's turn to be discussed, the last paragraph devoted to João and first to Pedro might read this way:

> . . . Maria Lourdes and João conquered their loneliness by doing the same favorite hobbies in the U.S. that they would have been doing back home. Pedro, on the other hand, spent most of his weekends mountain climbing with the Sierra Club. He had never seen a mountain in Belém, though plenty of piranhas, electric eels and vampire bats.

Again, study the examples in the publication where you want to appear. Copy the articles, then circle every word or phrase used to move the understanding or flow forward. See the pattern and phrases that provide natural, inconspicuous aids to readers who never want to have to go back to see how what they are reading fits into something said before.

Word choice and paragraph length

Word choice refers to the kinds of words you select, their direct relationship to the idea expressed and the readers being addressed and the comprehension level of that readership.

This is best seen when comparing an article in an academic journal to an article about the same subject in *USA Today*. Neither is "right." Each is appropriate for its purpose and readers. Erudite polysyllabic jawbreakers, in-house jargon and the orderly use of footnotes are the trademarks of academic publishing. *USA Today*, on the other hand, uses copy that is fast, clear, footnote-free and decidedly nonacademic, though not unintelligent.

Some jargon does find its way into commercial writing, which is appropriate when used correctly. It's far faster to tell baseball buffs that a hardball pitched too close to a batter's chin is a "duster" or a "headhunter" than to explain it in detail. They will know what a "whiff," "Texas Leaguer," "intentional pass," "bean ball" and "tipped foul" are. Those terms belong in baseball articles, add flavor and authenticity and distinguish the writer as either an insider or well researched. But calling a "Texas Leaguer" a "short fly ball that lands behind the infielder and in front of the outfielder" is "bush," as any insider knows.

One of the hardest things is knowing what level of words is appropriate for certain readers. This is important only at the earlier ages, when writing for pre-high schoolers and particularly for new readers. In that case, you should consult reading lists for the first grades of school (although obtaining them is difficult; schoolteachers might give you a copy of their list, if they in fact have one). The other way is, again, to read other articles written specifically to that level to get a feel for the degree of complexity and amount of abstraction those readers can handle. Remember too that topics taken for granted by adults—sex, suicide, divorce, mayhem or abstinence—will not be understood or of interest to youngsters, so editors won't buy them.

As for paragraph length, most paragraphs should be about the same length as the lead: a sentence or two long, sometimes three but rarely four. Editors break up large blocks of copy because they impede reading flow and intimidate the reader. Favor the newspaper approach: two sentences maximum. (Don't believe it? Find a newspaper and start counting!) The old rule was that at six agate lines (each $\frac{1}{14}''$) of copy it was time for another paragraph. Agates are gone but not the common sense behind the rule.

Again, study the magazines you are interested in writing for. You'll find their needs are different from school essays, which most new writers use as their models of form. In school one could write paragraphs until the subject or the writer expired. Not so in commercial writing. After a couple of sentences, it's time for a new paragraph. Write an article that can be quickly read and understood by the reader. Break up the material with quotes or anecdotes. Keep your descriptions tight and short, if needed at all. Count the number of sentences per paragraph, determine the average, then stick close to it.

The conclusion

The conclusion is important in magazine or longer newspaper feature pieces. Yet it's the least important element of a regular newspaper article, where the editor cuts from the bottom up. (About the first thing journalism students learn is the "inverted pyramid" style—which means that everything vital is at the top, with the rest inserted in descending order of importance. That way, if the last couple of paragraphs get snipped, the loss is minimal.) News pieces simply run out when they end. The conclusion of most magazine or feature articles usually reinforces what their leads promise. If it's a patriotic piece, the conclusion should compel you to rise to salute. If nostalgia is its theme, you should have a lump in your throat when you read the last word. You get the idea.

But there's another "old writer's trick" to conclusions, particularly for those pieces that are hard to end with impact or purpose: If you are having trouble finding a tight, clear, reinforcing ending, look for a word or a phrase in the lead that can be comfortably repeated in the final paragraph. (You've seen this a hundred times and probably never paid any attention to it. Now it will jump out at you every time it's done!) This creates the sense of having gone full circle, of a journey completed—just don't force it. And don't reuse something from the title. Since editors so often change your title, a reference to it in the conclusion, if it's not used, won't make any sense.

The title

As mentioned above, in a newspaper piece your title may never be used, since it must be set in headline form to fit the column dimensions. And half the time magazine editors will chuck out your words of genius for something more mundane. But you still have to call the article something, so do your best to give it a title that works and will stick.

Think of a title as the first lead, though only a few words long, that will make the reader want to see more of what you have written. That title pulls the reader to the actual lead, which continues to pull them into the body. Once there, studies show, the reader will finish the article if it sustains interest and doesn't have a large copy block that obstructs easy comprehension.

A good title tells what the article is about, often as directly as possible. In humor, it must reflect the same degree and kind of humor as the text. If the article is dry and wry, a twist of the same is called for in the title. If it's a thigh-slapper, the title had better be equally as funny. Editors rarely change humor titles, so attention is vital there.

The best humor titles, incidentally, come from the heart of the material—never the lead—and are therefore written last. Finish your article, write a dozen titles and try them on your friends. Ask them what they think the article is about. No inside jokes in the title, though.

The mechanics of article submission

Let's start with a presumption editors would heartily applaud: Your article would have to be exceptional—extraordinary is more accurate—to overcome lousy packaging and marketing. Conversely, bring the packaging and marketing up to standard and any copy has a far better chance of being bought. That's particularly important for beginners whose first copy is more likely good than exceptional or extraordinary. Poor presentation of a good idea is a liability you cannot afford at the outset or at any time.

Do you recall the earlier suggestion that, at any stage, you pose as a professional while you earn the credentials? Where form is concerned, make the pose believable by doing what professionals do: Offer clean copy, on-time delivery, names and labels where they should be and so on. (Yes, there are professionals who submit like slobs and seem to break every rule. They are tolerated, not loved. Do as they do, if you must, after your hundredth sale.)

Here are the standards, or rules if you need rules.

Paper

Submit the final draft on standard size (8½″×11″) white paper, one side only. Twenty-pound copier paper is fine. You can staple newspaper submissions (since they get rougher handling), but paper clips are better for magazines. For books, put the entire book in a box—the kind you get at copy shops works well.

Preparation

If you are preparing your copy on a computer, use serif type, such as Times Roman. (You are reading serif type now.) Avoid any form of script or anything else that's hard to read. Print the final, clean draft on a letter-quality printer. (Incidentally, if you're not using a computer, you are spending far too much time editing and composing on a typewriter. Used computers abound for as little as $100.)

Don't run your words from one edge of the page to the other. Fifteen spaces for the left margin (or 2″ from the left side of the paper) is enough for the editor to write in any instructions; leave about 1½″ unjustified on the right side. (If your computer has 1″ borders on the page setup, put your margins at 1 and 7, with the indent at 1½.) Use type no smaller than 10 points, but 11 or 12 are better. Double- or triple-space.

Start the copy halfway down your first page. At the top of that page, type the title in capital letters. Don't underline it or put quotation marks around it unless they are needed to indicate a nickname or other special designation. Center the title in the middle of the top half of page one. About three lines below it, also centered, type "by" followed by your name. (That is your "byline.") In the upper right corner, write the approximate word count, rounded off to the closest 25. You can handwrite the number in after the manuscript is completely typed and you've checked the word count. Each word counts. Even short words.

Leave a lot of white space at the bottom. If you want the typesetter to leave white between sections of your copy, skip about five lines and type the space symbol (#) in the center of that white opening. Don't suffocate your editor with too much copy per page; surround the text with plenty of blank paper.

Don't leave "widows," single lines at the bottom or top of a page. It used to be because typesetters would miss them and turn your copy into senseless babble. But since most copy now is finally submitted on disk (as will soon be explained), the strongest reason is because newspaper editors, trained in precomputer days, particularly disliked them for the reason stated—an important point since most magazine editors started with newspapers.

Put at least your name and address on every page. You can use a one-line footer, like that following (boxed here for emphasis), or you can buy address stickers and adhere them in the lower right corner.

> Ima Writer, 123 5th St., Punctuation, IL 60666, (212) 778-1345/fax (212) 778-1346

At the top of each inside page, about an inch down and another inch above the copy, you can insert a header that includes the title or an abbreviated form in capital letters, your name in the usual upper- and lowercase and the page number. For example:

> SINGING TURTLES, Writer, 2

On the last page of copy, a few lines below the last words, type one of three things (but not all three): (1) the word END, (2) -30- (a printer's symbol meaning there is nothing more to follow) or (3) # # #.

Punctuation

Two punctuation problems plague new writers. One, semicolons; use them rarely, but correctly. A high school primer will explain how. Two, learn how to use dashes, which means an em dash without spaces before or after it. If you're working on a computer, refer to your software manual—it will show how to access this character, which doesn't appear on a standard keyboard. A dash on your typewriter, incidentally, is two hyphens. Never end a typed manuscript line with a hyphen, even if it looks odd to carry the whole word to the next line. Carry it over, with the editor's blessing.

Those are the usual needs and problems. Common sense and editors' eyesight rule. Remember, if the copy is extraordinary, you get some leeway. But why take the chance when it's easier to do the whole package consistently right?

Mailing your manuscript

Mailing the article! What a relief! You want your manuscript to arrive as quickly as possible, flat, intact and undamaged—to receive a response with the same positive haste.

Some guidelines for mailing

If you want the manuscript plus a reply letter or note back, you must include a SASE (self-addressed, stamped envelope). The envelope should be the same size as the original envelope, folded in half with the stamps already affixed. If you don't want the manuscript back, as may be the case with simultaneous submissions, a small stamped envelope should be included that is large enough to hold a reply.

If you send items abroad, or even to Canada, you have three choices: (1) find out the cost and kind of stamps of that country needed to return your reply, get them (perhaps through the embassy or consulate), and put them on the return envelope; (2) include the right number of international reply coupons (IRCs) if you can find anybody at the Post Office who knows how many are required; or (3) leave stamps off the envelope and count on any interested editors to provide them for positive replies. In fact, the third approach works pretty well. No reply, no interest. If the copy is sufficiently exciting, they seem willing to foot a buck or two to let you know. There's a fourth way: Put your e-mail and fax numbers on your letter and invite them also to respond that way.

Don't send manuscripts in report covers or binders.

Cover letters should be sent with simultaneous submissions, of course, as was explained in chapter eight. They may be necessary for single submissions that are not preceded by a query, like fillers or humor, but only if you have something to say: your writing background, special expertise in the subject and so on. Don't just say you want the editor to buy the piece. She knows.

Rarely do you need a cover letter for queried articles or books, unless there is something special in the contents or that has occurred since the query that affects the manuscript. Don't try to sell at that point. Let the copy do the work.

The outside wrapping should be sturdy enough to protect the work against rough handling in transit. It should be tightly sealed and include both your return address and the name of a person, with address, where it is being sent. If you don't know the proper name, you can send it to the appropriate editor: Articles Editor, Managing Editor, etc. If the piece is six pages or fewer, you can fold it like a regular letter and send it in a business envelope. Anything larger should be sent flat.

A book manuscript sent unbound in a box should include a return address tag and sufficient stamps for its return, which are paper clipped to the top of the manuscript. Book publishers rarely reuse the same box and never the same wrapping.

There are less expensive ways to ship or mail, but priority or first class is the best. The item arrives in a few days, will be returned if the publication folded while you were gathering the facts and words and gets far less mauling. Write "PRIORITY MAIL" or "FIRST CLASS" in giant letters on the wrapping so it gets sent that way. Forget insurance. Just keep a copy of everything you mail, and should it go astray—it almost never happens, despite the usual grumbling about the postal service—you can mail another copy.

Most editors feel that certified or registered mail isn't worth the expense. Some resent it, thinking it signals trouble ahead—the writer thinks the editor will steal the work and never pay so the signature of receipt will serve for later litigation. Alas, it is usually signed for, if at all, by the mail clerk!

Keeping track of your mailing

Make a point of logging everything you mail out: the query letters, simultaneous submissions, photos and slides, plus all the details that come from mailing and the resulting responses.

The simple mailing record that follows will prevent you from sending the same query or manuscript to the same editor more than once. It serves as proof of your volume of work for an IRS audit, reminds you which editors have not replied, which are prompt and buy often, and how much income you are earning from your writing.

These eight points will help you set up your own mailing record:

1. So you can tell at any time where your article or book manuscripts are, what steps you have taken to sell them and if they have sold or are pending, a mailing record is extremely helpful.

2. This might be kept on loosely assembled sheets of paper or in memory on a computer hard disk or a removable floppy disk.

3. If kept on loosely assembled sheets of paper, on the top of each page write the year and the respective page number after it—1996 (7)—and keep these assembled with the last page on top to the first on the bottom. If the paper is 8½″ × 11″, list about six items per page with an inch or two between each listing so you can itemize each subsequent step taken.

4. To tell the status of each submission at a glance, you may wish to record your entries in this or a similar fashion:

   a. If the manuscript is rejected, cross through it with a colored felt pen. Use a see-through color such as yellow or pink so you can tell which publication rejected it and you don't inadvertently submit to the same company again!

   b. If an editor asks to see the manuscript as a result of your query, or anything else of a positive nature that might lead to its purchase, place brackets on both sides of the entry to indicate "positive reply and in process."

   c. Also use brackets when an editor who pays on publication indicates that your manuscript is being held or considered and there is reasonable expectation that it could be bought.

   d. If your manuscript is bought, or accepted by a publication that pays on acceptance, box the entire submission to show it is a pending purchase. If accompanied by a check, or when it arrives, write the date of its arrival and circle the amount of that check next to it.

   e. All related action is written below the manuscript's listing, in chronological order, so you can follow its development.

   f. An example of how your mailing record might appear follows, showing (1) a rejected query letter, (2) a request to see the manuscript from a submitted query, (3) a newspaper travel piece being held, and (4) a purchased manuscript from a query, with all related activities and a check received.

1996 (7)

~~6/17 — Q - Christmas Parade in Carpinteria - *Happiness Magazine*~~

6/17 — Q - Walking Guidebook of Downtown in San
Antonio - Finn Books

    7/2 - Send three chapters (1, 4, 6) plus 20
sample colored slides; needs by 9/25.
Also estimated book length, # of
photos

6/18 — Minneapolis Skywalk - *San Ignacio Reporter*

    7/14 - Holding for use in July, send b/w pix
    7/15 - Sent 16 b/w's, proofs with captions

6/18 — Q - Tulsa's Updated Downtown YMCA -
Oklahoma Magazine

    7/5 - Send ms, plus slides and b/w's
    7/17 - Sent ms, 24 slides, 30 b/w's
    8/3 - Accepted ms, 2 slides, 2 b/w's
    8/15 - $420

---

5. If kept in computer memory, identify as MSMAIL.96 (or the respective year). You may wish to create a template for fast, consistent listing. Instead of crossing through rejections or using brackets or boxes to indicate the current status, simply code each listing by a symbol inserted before the date. If no response,

no symbol. If rejected, (-) is typed before the date. If being held with a positive expectation of purchase, (+). And if bought, ($). Remember to copy the file regularly for safekeeping.

6. The mailing record is used both to record the status of submissions and for tax purposes, to indicate the volume of business conducted during the tax year, the number of queries sent, the sales made and the income generated.

7. A filing system for all paperwork related to the submissions on the mailing record must also be maintained. It contains a paper copy of all query letters, manuscripts and related correspondence sent; all query responses and related paperwork received; all paper research and anything else gathered that relates to the manuscript.

8. Your mailing record should be updated daily, or every time there is a change of status.

CHAPTER TEN

Copyright and Other Rights— Including the Internet

The last thing you want to do is write some masterpiece, then find it in print somewhere else under another byline. Or in that same publication, after it has been rejected. Or have it appear and not get paid.

Don't fret. Horror stories abound in the "stolen" copy arena, but almost all of them are the same old stories debearded, re-frocked and retold. If there ever was a grain of truth to them, it has become a boulder in the retelling.

The minuscule remainder are built on some substance, again probably magnified for dramatic effect or to double-tweak your sense of compassion—writers thrive on tweaked compassion. If something you write gets stolen once or twice in a lifetime, it's a bit like getting your pocket picked or hearing your only original joke getting laughs at a party, told by somebody else! You can take precautions, as you'll see in this chapter. But you can't afford to develop a howling paranoia about it. Big deal: Write something else that really *is* worth stealing.

I've had far more than 1,600 articles in print (I've stopped counting, frankly) and fifteen books. Twice I saw ideas I presented in a full query on the same editor's pages written by somebody else about four months later. Probably plucked in toto and suggested to a writer the editor knew. And five times editors put my copy in print and failed to pay within a year. Maybe .1 percent (1/1000th) of my income kept by cheats—any other businessperson would drool at those figures. What did I do about it? In two cases a complaint to the Better Business Bureau closest to the publication resulted in full payments. Two others folded with my work in their last issues. One of those brought a $.17 check on a bankruptcy settlement of a $50 claim. The fifth still owes me $150, an eighteen-year debt I may have to forget. But you still have to protect your rights and your words: They are your own creation and the only tangible thing you have to hold on to when the flurry of creativity subsides.

If you can set aside the paranoia, all that remains is clarifying the concepts, telling you how to protect yourself as best you can and then dipping into the newly emerging miasma of who should get paid (and usually doesn't) when your magazine or newspaper text suddenly appears on the Internet. That is, you must understand the different kinds of rights, how you can protect yourself and what to do if you see your work in print—and you haven't been paid.

Two kinds of rights are involved in freelance sales. The most discussed is *copyright*. That protects the words as they are written. The second is what puts the food on the table; it is called *contractual rights*, and includes *all rights*, *first rights* and *second rights*. (There are no "third rights"—or more.) The last rites you don't want to sell to a publisher. While copyrights and contractual rights sound perplexingly similar, they are distinct in purpose and means of procurement. Let's discuss each separately—after a disclaimer. I'm not a lawyer, and if you have specific questions about any of the rights discussed, you should seek legal counsel.

Copyright

Copyright is a scary concept to many writers, yet nothing could be more straightforward or easier to register. Nor is any term more often misused when applied to writing. The standard question is, "Did you copyright your book—or article or script?" In fact, the only sensible question is whether you *registered* the copyright.

The United States is a common-law country. In it the rights to the copy come with its creation. As you write an article or take notes in a class, when you "fix" a mode of expression in "copy" (words), that copy is "copyrighted" as it is written. The rights to that copy are automatically yours. By giving written form to an idea, you are creating property—no less than if you were sculpting a statue, painting on a canvas or placing original note combinations on a score. In each case the rights to that property are yours *as you give it form*, without need of further legal action. (It has nothing to do, either, with the quality of the product: Amazingly, atrocious drivel enjoys the same lofty legal ownership as your magnificent meanderings.)

Should somebody else take your property, sell it and cause you financial damage, you could take them to court. All that the judge would need to know would be who wrote the material in that form first. But proving who wrote the material first is not always easy—that's where establishing your copyright comes in.

The beauty of both the selling process that this book describes— query letters mailed, manuscripts submitted, copies kept, mailing records and the copyright process itself—is that you will have recorded a paper trail establishing clear dates of existence.

To register or not

Why not just put the symbol on everything and register it? First, it costs money and time; second, it can be counterproductive.

The only reason to register a copyright is to protect the financial value or earning power of the copy. But protecting your intellectual property is not always that easy. If somebody takes your copy and makes money from it, as the final step you would take her to court through an infringement suit. Such suits are expensive. Many items frankly aren't valuable enough to justify going to court. The cost of victory would be more than the settlement. So only the potentially lucrative forms of creation usually get registered: books, scripts, music, lyrics, newsletters and software for computers. For articles, it's up to you.

The symbol can be counterproductive because most magazine and newspaper editors (at least those I know) don't expect you to copyright articles or put the symbol on them. They know the rights are yours. The symbol so offends a few of them that they will refuse even to read it. They see it as a foolish flag of paranoia, if not a red flag signaling litigious troubles ahead. It says to them that you think they will steal your words and not pay.

In fact, editors would be fools to put your words in print without payment, as they know. Nor do 99 percent have the slightest interest in doing so.

Why might you consider registering the copyright on your article nonetheless? Because it may lose its identity with you if later used on the Internet. With such uses poorly defined at the present, the symbol (or its absence) might give you an extra edge in future negotiation or litigation. More on the Internet to follow.

Registering the copyright for a book is strongly advised unless another publisher is securing the copyright for you in your name after the text sees light (as almost all do). Complete and submit the registration forms once the copy is in final, printed form.

The process of copyright registration

When it makes sense to register your copyright, how do you do it? Send the properly completed application forms, a fee for each application and two complete copies of the best edition of published works—or one copy of unpublished work—to the Register of Copyrights, Copyright Office, Library of Congress, Washington, DC 20559. The copyright symbol should be affixed to the item before it is sold or distributed publicly. Then you have up to a year to complete the registration once that item is sold or distributed. In certain cases you can also include many items of a similar nature on the same form for the same fee. The date of creation is established when you file. A litigant would have to prove that he wrote the book before your registration date. That's a giant legal difference.

How must the symbol be displayed? For literary items, it is a © followed by the date of creation and the writer's name. The symbol tells others that according to the Copyright Act of 1976 (title 17, U.S. Code) you, as the owner of the copyright, have the exclusive right to do and authorize others to do the following:

- *to reproduce* the copyrighted work in copies
- *to prepare derivative works* based upon the copyrighted work
- *to distribute copies* of the copyrighted work to the public by sale or other transfer of ownership, or by rental, lease, or lending

- *to perform the copyrighted work publicly*
- *to display the copyrighted work publicly*

You can register literary works, musical works (including words), dramatic works (including music) and motion pictures and other audiovisual works.

Some other key points about copyright directly from the explanatory booklet:

> For works created (fixed in tangible form for the first time) after January 1, 1978, the term of (copyright) protection starts at the moment of creation and lasts for the author's life, plus an additional 50 years after the author's death. (This differs for joint or group authorship and for works made for hire.)
>
> Under the 1976 Act, a work of original authorship is protected by copyright from the time the work is created in a fixed form; registration with the Copyright Office is not a condition of copyright protection itself (except to preserve a copyright if a work has been published with a defective or missing copyright notice), but copyright registration is a prerequisite to an infringement suit.
>
> The old law required, as a mandatory condition of copyright protection, that the published copies of a work bear a copyright notice. The new enactment calls for a notice on published works, but omission or errors will not immediately result in loss of the copyright, and can be corrected within certain time limits. Innocent infringers misled by the omission or error will be shielded from liability.
>
> For copyright questions, call (202) 707-3000 any time for a recorded message, 8:30-5:00 ET Monday to Friday to speak to a specialist. For forms, call (202) 707-9100.

You can no more copyright ideas than you can put a fence around the wind. The wind (like an idea) belongs to everybody. What is unique is how you express those ideas; *that* is the copyrightable element. Writing about pig farming doesn't prevent others from either doing it or writing about it, in general or in particular. Your rights are limited to what you say precisely as you say it: the words in the order they are stated, whether they are correct, brilliant, barbled or suspect. Others can write about the same topic, cite the same examples, use your facts, even use the same words—but the order had better be different or they are stepping squarely in the middle of your rights, registered or not.

Contractual rights

Of more pecuniary importance are the rights that are purchased with your manuscript. Those are contractual rights. They define how often the editor can use your copy and are part of the three-element definition of contract: offer, consideration and acceptance.

You want to sell your writing to an editor, yet you must know what you are selling, when and the limits to how it can be used. Copyright provides a general legal framework for your protection, at the national and international levels. The contractual rights are specific to you and the publisher securing permission to use the text.

You write a query letter: "Would you be interested in buying an article about . . . ?" Or you submit a finished manuscript. Either is an offer. Consideration refers to money. Since the pay rates of most publications are listed in the current *Writer's Market*, or that information is readily available and it is generally understood anyway that commercial publications pay for manuscripts used, consideration is in this relationship generally understood as being implied and need not be mentioned in the correspondence or transaction. (If there was any doubt at the time I was dealing with the editor, however, I'd mention it, and if doubt still persisted, get it in writing.)

What remains is the acceptance. We have discussed various forms of acceptance and rejection in this book, but for our needs now the editor must at some point agree that the article will be bought. Somewhere between the offer and that acceptance, you should know the rights that will be purchased.

Usually that is simple. The *Writer's Market* entry will state: "Buys all rights" or "Buys first North American serial rights" or whatever. (Serial means magazine.) If that is acceptable, no mention of rights need be made in your correspondence. As long as the edition of that guide is current, you can expect those rights to be bought. (Again, if it's unclear or you want absolute confirmation, explain this to the editor.) If nothing is stated concerning the rights, ask.

These rights fall into three general categories: all rights, first rights and second rights.

All rights

Some of the highest-paying publications want all rights (yet many of those will settle for first rights). "All rights" is as comprehensive as it sounds. The publication buys all the rights to what you wrote, to use as it sees fit, in the first printing, subsequent printings, anthologies and so on. Sounds dreadful until you realize that all the editors bought was the expression of an idea as written. Those words in that order. They can make modest editorial changes in the text, but their use is limited essentially to what you provided. They didn't buy the idea, nor can they prevent you from using that idea elsewhere in another fashion or in other words.

So all rights is far less restrictive than it implies, and it always pays the best. If an editor wants to buy all rights and the pay is good, you are faced with two choices.

One, sell it and simply rewrite the idea for other markets. The change must be significant: a new title, lead, quotes and conclusion. A better way is to find a different slant or approach and write a different article altogether. Facts are reusable, ideas can't be embargoed and an all-rights buy can indeed be all right!

On the other hand, to rewrite the piece puts you in direct competition with the magazine that bought the first version, however modest or great your changes, since the topic is essentially the same. You are in the business of creating properties and renting them, so why give this away when, with a bit of resistance, the editor will probably buy first rights anyway. Here you say no, that the first rights only are for sale.

First rights

Magazines usually purchase first rights—the rights to have it appear first in that form on their pages. No surprises, so it doesn't pop up in the competition three days before it sees light on their pages.

It's a better deal for you too since the very same article without a word's change can be sold again and again, after it has been in print. The key word is *after*. Once sold, every subsequent sale becomes a reprint or second rights sale.

What do you do if an editor buys it and doesn't use it? Can you sell that manuscript again? Not right away. After a reasonable period of time, which could be from several months to a year, contact the editor and ask when the manuscript is going to be used or whether the publication would return the rights to you. (If it does, you keep the money. You sold it in good faith. The publisher's decision not to use it was just that, *his* decision.) If he returns it to you, you can then sell first rights to another editor. You needn't mention the piece's selling history.

A good way to avoid that dilemma is to insert a deadline in the contract stating that if the article is not published within a year after delivery, the right to publish it is automatically lost, unless extended by mutual agreement. That way you needn't ask or wait. No article, one year, it's yours again to sell for the second first time!

Second rights

The minute a first-rights sale hits the stands, you can sell the article again, as is or modified, as second or reprint rights, unless there is an exclusivity period in your contract. We'll discuss reprints and rewrites fully in chapter twelve so we can clarify both the marketing and mailing issues concerning reselling at one time.

The rights issue is easy enough to grasp. Reprints almost never have exclusivity—in that rarest of rare cases that an editor does want some exclusivity, that decision is yours. In almost all cases, the article was printed and the buyer purchased first rights. By appearing in print, the buyer used those rights. You can send the same article to more editors once it has seen light, as long as you tell those editors (1) who bought first rights, (2) when and where it appeared in print and (3) that you are offering reprint (or second) rights. They should then know that there is no exclusivity and that they have one-time rights to material their readers may have already seen in print.

What do you do if you see your item in print elsewhere— or you don't get paid?

This begs some precedence questions.

If you sent a query and it was rejected and then the idea appears in print much as you proposed it, that is one problem. Let's call it A.

If you sent a full manuscript and it was rejected and then the same words appear in print, that's a more serious problem. Let's call it B.

And if your article was sold to an editor, was printed and now reappears in another publication without the publisher having contacted you or made a payment, that's C.

Problem A, again, is if you sent a query and it was rejected, but the idea appears in print much as you proposed it.

That is irksome but probably insoluble. And surprisingly rare. What you don't know is whether the editor had another article very similar to yours being written or a query just like yours in hand. Or whether, as you suspect, your idea was shuttled to a hungry writing friend to whip quickly into shape. The editor isn't likely to fess up.

If the editor is above board and some of your query was used to modify or create an article, sometimes you will be paid for the idea or assistance in developing an idea. But that, too, is rare.

You should bring it to the editor's attention if only to see what happened. Do it in a nonthreatening way in writing, indicating your surprise and disappointment, explaining in detail where your query and the final piece so closely overlapped. That would put the editor on notice not to do it again, without saying as much. The editor would also have an opportunity to explain what happened if there was an overlap of articles about the same idea, or to apologize and make a modest payment. At least it doesn't irreparably damage future query submissions, if you wish to work with that editor later. (It might even make the editor more inclined to give your next query extra consideration.)

Idea stealing is hard to prove or prevent. The problem is the ephemeral, free-flowing nature of ideas themselves. They can't be chained up or fenced in or even kept intact, so fluid are they that in a moment one breaks into two, and those drift into a dozen more and so on. Ideas become property only when expressed in tangible forms and aired through means such as articles and books.

And how do you prove that the editor and you didn't have the same idea at the same time? Alexander Graham Bell and Elisha Gray not only invented telephones, completely unknown to each other, but they patented their inventions the very same day half a country apart!

It's a sobering thought that there may be far more writers stealing ideas from each other and pawning them off as originals as there are editors not paying for ideas converted into copy.

Think up another idea. A day or week of concentrated idea-thinking could fill a lifetime's larder. The thought that one idea of a hundred might be swiped from a query can be exasperating, but the only sane response is one of flash anger, resignation and submission—to another editor—of an even better idea.

One thing is certain: If you don't risk ideas, if you don't query or write articles or books, your writing future and income will be bleak. So take the gamble. Virtually all will be responded to, rejected or left for you to turn into copy. Chalk up the rest to man's perversity.

Problem B, where you sent a full manuscript and it was rejected and then the same words appeared in print, is indeed a more serious problem, but it's also very rare. It probably will be resolved in your favor without having to use legal force.

If your manuscript, written after a query go-ahead (or directly submitted to a simultaneous submission market), was rejected, you have the rejection letter. (If the editor simply didn't respond after you sent the manuscript, you should have sent a registered letter several months later stating that because of nonresponse you are withdrawing the manuscript for use.)

Make a copy of the printed article, your original query and the editor's go-ahead (or your registered manuscript withdrawal letter) and mail them to that editor with a letter thanking her for using your copy (including a reminder that the payment has yet to be received).

That should bring you a quick check and perhaps a note of apology. But if it brings silence, find out the name of the highest authority in the publishing firm (by calling or through the library)—preferably the chairman of the board—and send a copy of everything you sent to the editor with an additional note that you have *still* not received payment and hope that the recipient of this second letter will be able to resolve this obvious breach of contract. That should do it.

If the letter to the top honcho brings no reply, contact the Better Business Bureau closest to that publication. The BBB will send you a form to complete to which you should attach a copy of all the above items. The BBB isn't a collection agency, but it does an excellent job of mediating. It will send your complaint to the company and will lend its good offices to prod the publisher into responding. At the same time—always sending a copy to the same top authority—you can contact the postmaster at the publication's ZIP code and explain the situation, asking whether the firm is still in business; write to *Writer's Digest*, the monthly counterpart to *Writer's Market*, explaining what happened; notify the editor of the newsletter of any writing organization you belong to, to share your experience with the readership; and contact consumer advocacy groups or representatives of the local newspaper and radio/TV stations that, by the same kind of negative publicity, get businesses to listen.

Still nothing? Small Claims Court, where you act as your own lawyer. Finally, the full lawsuit. You will rarely get beyond the first or second step before some resolution is made, if you have any case at all.

Problem C is a simple case of copyright infringement: Your article was sold to an editor and printed, and that article now reappears in another publication without the publisher having contacted you or made a payment.

Send a copy of the article in question, a copy of the article as it appeared in the original publication, a copy of your correspondence with that editor and an explanation that you were the author of the material in question and that this publication has printed it without authorization or payment. Would the publisher please make the payment at the standard rate by _____ date (give thirty days) so it isn't necessary to refer this to your attorney.

A check should be forthcoming. If it isn't, call that editor after the thirty days have passed. If it looks like you won't be paid, you can follow the path explained in problem B or jump directly to the Small Claims Court, then a lawyer. You should collect this check somewhere along the way.

The truth is that most editors need you and your ideas, are too busy and bright to play games with your words, know the legal consequences if they do, don't want to court either public disfavor or their own publishers' wrath and are simply honest, if not a bit poky in replying and imperfect in keeping you abreast of every step of an article's development. A relationship built on trust, open communication and a grain of patience on both parts makes problems like A, B and

C so rare that to a journeyman writer working the trade, they are at best a remote concern too distant to interrupt business as usual.

Work for hire

"Work for hire" is a term that has become much more prevalent in the past few years. It means that if somebody hires you to write (design, draw, photo, etc.) something for him on a work-for-hire basis, you will be paid solely for your labor. The resulting product belongs to the person who hired you and can be passed on to others. You have received your last payment. There will be no royalties or future compensation. Moreover, your product can be changed at will, and, unless you stipulate otherwise, your name can be attached to it in any mutation.

This is the usual way that firms work with employees for anything they create "on company time." Universities do the same. The thought is that since you are being paid to create, there should be no further payments for the creation. The copyright, likewise, belongs to your employer.

Work for hire becomes important to a freelancer in that subsequent sales, such as second rights, bring you no additional income. How do you know when you're in a work-for-hire relationship? It must say so, in so many words, in your signed contract or letter of agreement. If there is doubt, look for any reference to royalties or additional payments. In a work-for-hire contract, there won't be any.

A few publications work that way only, so if you are going to write for them, those are the conditions you must accept. The vast majority stipulate clearly if their purchases are for first rights, reprint rights or whatever. Sometimes newcomers are offered what is derisively called by other freelancers the "sucker contract." If they refuse to work on a work-for-hire basis, sometimes there appears a new contract with new conditions, usually first or second rights as the key feature.

Let's discuss electronic rights next since the multicontract issue and work for hire are very much at the heart of new circumstances that have arisen with the new technology.

Electronic rights

For years writers' biggest concern was their words leaking into another newspaper or magazine or sometimes sliding from one media to the other, and how they were going to get paid every time somebody stole or duplicated their brilliance. Then the Internet appeared and their fears became a reality: The very same words in the very same form were reappearing almost magically on monitors, then being down-loaded and reprinted, in every nook of the globe.

If that wasn't enough, CD-ROMs appeared and the same articles and books began appearing again—without acknowledgment or additional compensation.

Editors and publishers—some writers themselves and all posing as the writer's best friend—turned an occasional fiscal bruise into a gaping monetary sore. To which they turned their eyes skyward, shook their collective heads and said, in effect, "Sorry about that. Electronic rights? CD-ROMs? Nobody makes money from them. They're the new technology. They belong to everybody. Sorry, they came after you signed away your life. There will be no payment."

How did it happen that authors suddenly lost economic control of their creations? Much of it was work developed before the electronic changes, so it fell through the contract cracks. Some of the publishers had slipped in a clause that they owned the electronic rights. A few quietly switched to work-for-hire contracts. And almost all of the rest just wrote it off as an unfortunate coincidence of the times.

How did professional writers react? Some were unaware or uncon-cerned, and many of the newer writers were afraid that saying anything negative about a sale or contract would squelch the deal. Fortunately, a cadre of more seasoned writers, most members of writers organiza-tions, replied in a collective, "No way, José!" and started picking their new contracts apart, crossing off anything that didn't protect their rights, and writing in what they wanted.

Which is where the issue rests as this book is being composed—but with the future considerably brighter for all freelancers being paid for each use of their work in every format.

Some publishers immediately recognized the inequity and have drawn up new contracts usually offering a two-leveled payment, one for the work itself, the second for derivative use by electronic and other media. They then devised a format to pay modest, retroactive fees for earlier electronic use for works that had appeared without the writers' permission before the contract changes.

Other publishers agreed to pay through the new Authors Registry, a not-for-profit licensing and royalty collection agency for writers, which was formed in 1995 and is loosely modeled after the music world's ASCAP (American Society of Composers, Authors and Publishers), which was founded more than eighty years ago when, in a similar industry change, songs that had brought income only from sheet music sales began to yield royalties from radio, records and live performances.

Virtually every important writers group and nearly one hundred literary agencies (with members and clients totaling more than 50,000) have become cooperating organizations with the Authors Registry. Their members are eligible to enroll without charge. Unaffiliated writers may join as individuals for $10. (For more information from the Authors Registry, call (212) 563-6920, e-mail registry@interport.net, or see http://www.webcom.com/registry on the World Wide Web.)

Yet the vast majority of U.S. publishers are still wrestling with the issue, so you should read very carefully any contract offered to see how electronic rights are worded, after checking for *work for hire* and the rights being purchased. If the publication agrees to compensate you for additional use of your article or book and the rate seems reasonable, sign.

How do you address the issue if it isn't to your satisfaction, without losing the sale? You can ignore it and hope the publisher will compensate you retroactively if she makes a change. You can cross out any loss of those rights, write in "to be negotiated" and take your chances. You could do the same and indicate "payment to be made retroactively according to future contract changes for electronic rates." Or you could join a writers organization actively pursuing this issue and seek the group's advice before returning the contract.

CHAPTER ELEVEN

Writing and Taxes

The beauty of writing with the intent of earning income is that you can deduct almost all of your expenses, including travel, computers and postage from your taxable income. To do so, you must faithfully report your earnings, keep receipts and records of your expenditures, then itemize and deduct them.

Don't panic. You needn't rent a storefront, have stationery printed and join the Chamber of Commerce. You simply must do things in a businesslike way and, at least at the outset, submit a Schedule C with your annual 1040 federal tax form. Filing a Schedule C won't automatically bring an auditor to your door. If it did, our government would need a million auditors. It won't change a thing—unless you claim $300,000 in expenses for the sale of a $30 poem.

What follows is general advice culled from personal experience, talks with IRS employees while preparing a similar segment about taxes for my writing seminars, interviews with professional tax preparers and other books discussing the same topic. Still, because federal (and state) tax regulations change from time to time, and your particular situation may differ from the general conditions discussed, you should seek specific advice from the IRS or a tax consultant. (You have just read another disclaimer!)

Since most people will read this chapter seeking information about deductions, and we have no way of knowing about your specific state and local tax demands, the focus here will be on federal income tax, the deductions allowed on your federal return (which almost all of the states likewise accept) and recordkeeping.

But first you need to decide on the purpose of your writing.

If your purpose is simply to tinker with words now and then, all for the fun of it and with no serious intent to sell what you create, you have a hobby (for which you pay all the expenses and lose virtually all the tax deductions). But if your purpose is to earn income, to sell what you write, even though you have fun in the doing, your expenses are deductible. Which raises two key questions: How do you prove that purpose, and how do you show the expenses?

Proof of purpose

Proof of your purpose becomes necessary only if you are asked, probably at an audit (which is unlikely unless your tax return looks blatantly unbusinesslike, you are excessively greedy, you are dishonest or you doggedly report losses long after you should be showing gains).

If proof of purpose is called for, there are two important items that will show income-earning intent. One is volume of output. The second is letters of intent.

The first you prove by maintaining a mailing record of every letter and manuscript sent to potential buyers. If all such submissions are kept in chronological order, and the pages are held together with brads or a clip, the volume of transactions will be readily available to show upon request.

In addition, retain copies of every manuscript or letter mailed during the year, plus all responses (including mass-produced rejection forms on which you should note what was rejected and when it was sent). Don't paste rejections on your wall unless you want to take your wall to the audit!

Clearly there must be some evidence of seriousness of purpose in the volume of items offered for sale. If you send out one query letter every few months, plus an article a year, the volume will scarcely distinguish your income-earning from a hobby. And if you try to deduct several thousand dollars of expenses against such an underwhelming marketing volume, your deductions may well be denied.

Letters of intent are more a term than an actual thing. That is, except in the rarest of occasions, there is no such thing as a letter clearly identified or labeled as a "letter of intent." Rather, these are positive replies to query letters. Often they are notes scribbled on the queries themselves saying, "Let's see it" or "Send on spec."

What the editor is saying in giving you a positive response to a query is, "I seriously intend to consider purchasing the copy you will prepare for me for publication." Thus, based on that intent, you can deduct all reasonable expenses incurred in its preparation.

This is because the editor cannot make a purchasing decision without reading the final copy, and you must pay certain expenses to gather information, write and submit that final manuscript. It isn't essential that the editor buy the article for you to deduct reasonable costs. It is important only that you have queried in professional business fashion, received a positive response and sent a final manuscript for full consideration.

A critical word in this deduction is "reasonable," for which there are as many definitions as "letters of intent." A $5,000 trip to Borneo to write a $50 article transcends reasonableness, at least where deductions are concerned. But $1,200 in costs for a $500 article may not be if the material gathered can be used for rewrites and reprints to earn three or four times the initial costs. Let common sense and the IRS be your guides.

Keeping track of deductible expenses

To report your earnings and expenses, use Schedule C (Profit or Loss From Business) of your Form 1040 (U.S. Individual Income Tax Return), submitted at regular filing time. It is self-explanatory, yet it can be confusing. (See "Using Schedule C" on page 195 for more information.) You may also need forms for depreciation (Form 4562) and computation of your Social Security Self-Employment Tax (Schedule SE), if either are applicable.

Just keep a sensible account of your writing-related income and expenses as they occur, tally them up at year's end and adjust your 1040 by inserting the figures appropriately.

It's imperative you keep receipts for money spent. Keeping track can be done one of four ways: (1) paying by check, of which you have a copy returned with your statement or held at the bank should you need to get a copy later; (2) paying by credit card, for which, again, you have a receipt as well as the monthly reconciliation form; (3) paying by cash and getting a receipt from the person to whom you make the payment; and (4) for nonreceipted items, by using a pocket booklet, a notebook in your glove compartment or purse or any sheet of paper where you make the notation of the amount, to whom and why. You may wish to keep a separate checking account and a distinct credit card, just for writing-related expenses, to simplify verification at tax time.

There are a few exceptions. Beyond tips, coin phones and small change items, food costs can be averaged on trips (or a per diem established) if they are reasonable: a certain amount for breakfast, lunch and dinner. Each year the IRS releases a current list stipulating the allowable per diem per city in the U.S., which you can secure by phone or in person.

Some other items are clearly deductible, if receipted and used to earn income by writing, for example, the necessary tools: paper, envelopes, pencils and pens. Buy stamps at the post office so you can get a receipt. Depreciate your word processor, hardware and software (or your typewriter). Deduct the toners, ribbons, correction liquid, repair and other supplies and direct costs.

If you use your telephone for writing-related purposes, deduct those calls (excluding the base rate). Cameras and tape recorders are depreciable, and film, tape, needed supplies and inexpensive accessories are normally deductible. Even a room in your house can provide numerous deductions if it is used exclusively as an office. You can request a booklet about this subject distributed free by the IRS. Use its method of calculating these deductions, which have become almost indecipherable.

Automobile expenses are best deducted on a per-mile basis (the IRS will give you the current figure) as long as they are logged regularly. A notebook stored in the glove compartment is perfect: Write the date, the miles traveled (or start/stop odometer readings) and how they pertain to writing. Other travel-related expenses are deductible—if reasonable and required. That includes getting to and from, food, lodging, tips, laundry and all other expenses needed to live and perform your task away from home. Entertainment, if directly related to writing income, can also be deducted.

It is far easier to justify the necessity of the travel if you have one or many letters of intent before you leave. Even query letters awaiting replies help since they show that the purpose of the trip mentioned is to write articles for publication.

What happens if you don't have letters of intent but simply take the trip and write when you return? You are usually limited to deducting proven and necessary expenses equal to the amount of money you earn. Or if you spend only a quarter of your time writing? You can deduct a maximum of 25 percent of your costs. Or if you spend a year elsewhere to learn a new culture so you can then write a novel with that setting? Keep receipts and take the deductions when the book is in print so you earn as much as you claim.

Keep in mind, though, that if you're just going to the library for the day, you can't even deduct your lunch! You must spend the night away to deduct meals, unless you are paying for another's meal as an entertainment expense. If you have to pay to park, use a copier or have a printout produced, though, those are deductible.

The best news? This book is deductible.

The worst news? You can't pay yourself a wage for writing.

You start taking deductions from the moment you incur expenses related to your writing income, even if the expenses precede that income. The IRS knows that a certain amount of "tooling up" is necessary for almost any business. You need a word processor or typewriter to submit query letters and manuscripts in readable fashion, for example. So it's perfectly conceivable to have many deductions without any income, and to have expenses exceed income for some months or even years while you perfect your marketing and writing skills.

But that can't continue forever—you must diligently seek a profit position in your writing activities and conduct your activities in a fashion conducive to earning a profit. A profit (more income than expenses) at least three of the first five years is the rough guideline. Nor can the expenses be vastly out of proportion to the potential earnings without drawing a stern challenge. Following a sensible, proven, businesslike process, as outlined in this book, should clearly distinguish your purpose and method as income oriented rather than as a hobby.

You will have many more questions concerning taxes. Horse sense and a close reading of materials easily obtainable from the Internal Revenue Service will answer 90 percent of them. Beyond that you may need a tax adviser or a professional preparer. Just remember that it is your duty, not just your opportunity, to claim every deduction that is rightly yours—but not a cent more.

Using Schedule C

If you are the sole owner of an unincorporated business, you must report business income and expenses on Schedule C (Form 1040). If you are making money or paying expenses or both, this is how you stay honest with everybody's uncle. Even if you have a regular job, or many jobs, you fill in one "C" for your writing. In addition, you must keep records and receipts for expenditures, plus copies of all correspondence (particularly queries and replies) and all submitted manuscripts.

Much of the form will not pertain to you if selling your writing is the limit of your activities. Part II, Cost of Goods Sold, has no bearing, nor will much of the other material on the back be applicable.

You don't need an employer identification number, line D, until you have employees (other than yourself); you can use your Social Security number, for identification. Nor must you have a business name, line C, other than your own. (In fact, if you do, you will want to complete the Fictitious Business Statement at your county records office.) Your address will likely be your home, unless you have a separate office. And most use "cash" as the accounting method in F. Part I, Income, is easy enough: List by source, then tally up the money received during that year from your writing. Include a copy of that list with your return, and keep a copy for your own records. Remember, that's actual money received (not promised, hoped for or talked about).

Part II, Expenses, is more fun at tax time. Alas, the Great Collector in Washington, DC, has no appreciation of creative talents, particularly in this area. He wants to see receipts, records, numbers, proof. So you should have been keeping these items together, to now lump by category, so you can receive benefit for having paid your business expenses.

The expenses you are most likely to have as a writer are bank service charges (if you keep your writing funds separate), car and truck expenses, depreciation (of equipment: word processor, printer, type-writer, cameras, etc.), dues and publications, office supplies and post-age, repairs, travel and entertainment, utilities and phone and inciden-tal costs. As your writing income increases, the number of categories will also increase.

Tally your income and your expenses. Subtract the smaller from the larger. If you made more than you spent, you have a profit. If not, you have a loss. Whichever, that is then posted on your regular 1040, from which the personal tax you owe is calculated.

Some IRS Suggestions That Apply to Writers

(Each item below comes directly from an IRS tax guide.)

1. Deposit all business receipts in a separate bank account and make all disbursements from that account by check. Avoid making out checks to cash. Rather, establish a petty cash fund for small expenditures.

2. Support all entries in that account with documentation. File all canceled checks, paid bills, duplicate deposit slips and other items that support entries in your books in an orderly manner and keep them in a safe place.

3. You must keep your business books and records available at all times for IRS inspection. They must be kept until the stat-ute of limitations for that return runs out—usually three years after the return is due or filed or two years from the date the tax was paid, whichever occurs later.

4. You may use a standard mileage rate instead of actual operat-ing and fixed expenses and depreciation for using your vehi-cle for business. Check the current rates with the IRS.

5. Parking fees and tolls paid during business use are also deductible.

6. Travel expenses are the ordinary and necessary expenses of foreign or domestic travel away from home for your busi-ness. Under that category deductible travel expenses include air, rail and bus fares; car expenses; fares or other costs of

local transportation; baggage charges and transportation; meals and lodging when you are away from home on business; cleaning and laundry; telephone and telegraph; public stenographer's fees; tips; and other, similar business-related expenses.

7. Entertainment expenses are usually deductible if they meet three criteria: (a) you had more than a general expectation of getting income or some other specific business benefit at some future time, and (b) you did engage in business with the person being entertained during the entertainment period, and (c) the main purpose of the combined business and entertainment was the business transaction.

Part Three

SELLING AGAIN AND AGAIN

CHAPTER TWELVE

Reselling Your Writing: Reprints and Rewrites

S elling an article once is a major accomplishment, at least while you're earning your spurs. Selling the same article again and again, or other articles derived from the same research, is utter delight.

How that is done is the purpose of this chapter.

For clarification, let's distinguish between the two major means of reselling.

The first, called "reprints," is in its simplest form the selling of the same article, as is, repeatedly to different markets.

The second, called "rewrites," is the taking of the same facts, quotes and anecdotes and reshuffling, expanding and rewriting them into new forms, each a different article using some or much of the same material.

Reprints

A traditional reprint sale follows the original sale of an article to an editor who purchased first rights. That editor bought the right to use your words, that article, in print first.

When those words appeared in print, the rights automatically reverted back to you, and your rights relationship with that editor ended.

What remained were second rights, which are also called reprint rights. (Second and reprint rights mean the same thing; the terms are interchangeable.)

Once your article has appeared in print from a first-rights sale, you can immediately offer that very same article, without change, to any other editor you think might buy it. It couldn't be more straightforward.

Writer's Market tells you the rights editors buy, or the editor will tell you when you receive a go-ahead to your query. The guide also tells whether the magazine pays on acceptance or publication.

Who buys second or reprint rights? Mostly editors who pay on publication, plus a few, whose readers would not likely have read your words in the first publication, who pay on acceptance.

How much do they pay? What they can get it for, or normally pay, since editors buying reprints have no idea what you originally received. Alas, those paying on publication aren't high rollers, and those paying on acceptance for a piece already used will recognize that you will sell for less (since you've already been paid for putting the research and words in final form), so figure a third to one-half of what the original purchaser paid, then consider it a boon if you make more.

The best thing about reprints is that through diligent and creative marketing, you can resell the same piece many times, so when the final tally is made, you might have earned more money for churning the same winning prose repeatedly than you made for selling the original.

Using dollars to reprove the point, if the original article took you eight hours to sell, research and write and paid you $450, that is a gross profit of $56.25 an hour. If you resell the same article three times, each paying $200 and taking forty-five minutes apiece to find the market, prepare a copy of the article, reprint the cover letter and get it in the mail, that is an additional $600, or $267 an hour. (You can substitute your own prep time and payment rates.)

Mind you, nobody has ever sold a reprint before he sold the original article, so the hard work—the idea finding, market picking, querying, editor studying, researching, writing, editing, rechecking and submitting—is done first. Reprints sold later are very tasty dessert to a hard-won meal.

So how do you get editors to buy reprints?

The reprint selling process

Sometimes editors feverishly seek you out, begging you to let them reuse a masterpiece you already sold—you name the price. (Or so I've heard from writers whose imaginations vastly exceed their credibility.)

Yet it does happen, on a far lesser scale. *Reader's Digest* and *Catholic Digest* are two well-known reprint magazines who do seek high-quality reprints to use (usually rewritten in a condensed form) on their pages. You can shorten their searches by sending copies of a particularly strong article with a cover letter suggesting they may wish to consider that recently published work for their pages.

There is no choice with the rest of the editors who might consider reusing your bought prose. You must find them, approach them in a sensible manner through a reprint cover letter and include a copy of the article in question and an SASE.

Finding the most likely reprint buyers

Common sense guides this search. Since you want to sell the reprint without change, comb *Writer's Market* to find other publications similar to that which originally printed your article. Check in the same subject category, or those with similar readerships. Start with the Table of Contents. Read carefully every publication that might even be remotely similar or use a topic like yours, as is or redirected to a different market or from a different setting.

Now create two columns on a sheet of paper. In the first column, write the title of every magazine that might use the article exactly as it is. Note the page number of the reference next to it, for easy finding later.

In the second column, write the title of every magazine that might use the subject if you rewrote or redirected it. Next to the name write down how you would have to rewrite the article to make it buyable: "for women: change examples, approach from female perspective," "wants history, focus on subject in early 1990s," "uses bullets: extract key points, create bullets," "change the setting to France, use French examples." Also include the source page number.

Let's focus on column one here, since the changes needed to rewrite the piece are obvious in column two.

You'll most likely want to contact the editors of all of the publications in column one, whether they pay on publication or acceptance. Once you've created a master reprint cover letter (see page 205), computers make it quick to customize the address and salutation and insert a personalized reference in the text. The potential of a resale, even slight, outweighs the small amount of time, copying and postage required to get your article and letter before a healthy scattering of eyes.

Do not send the reprint cover letter and article copy to those magazine editors paying on acceptance who already rejected your query, or to those major magazines that never buy second rights. Sometimes there are reprint buyers that are flat-out foes of each other. Submit to one first (the most likely to use it or pay the most), and the second if the first says no. (Years back I sold to the Air California and PSA magazines, both fierce competitors. While I was within my rights to simultaneously offer reprints to both, since reprint sales are nonexclusive, if both had bought the reprint and used it on their pages, I would have lost two good clients forever!)

Once you have identified your marketing targets, you'll need a clear copy of the article you want to sell as a reprint. If the article is exactly one page long and includes only your copy, great. Copy and send it as is. But when there is adjacent, nonrelated copy next to the text or the prose trickles onto later pages, you'll want to cut your article out and paste it up. Place the copy on an 8½" × 11" sheet of blank white paper, line it up and rubber-cement (or wax) it down. Include the photos or illustrations you also wish to sell. If the name of the publication and date of the issue aren't in the copy, add them to every page. And number the pages in consecutive order.

Then head to the quick copy shop to have as many copies reproduced as you will need, collated and stapled.

Just make certain the final copies you will send to the editors are clear, easy to read and include everything you want to be seen.

The reprint cover letter

It's not enough just to have names and addresses plus copies of what you want the editor to buy. You must sell the prospective buyer through a one-page cover letter accompanying the reproduced copy of the article.

Your cover letter must do five things:

1. It must make the topic come alive before the editor ever reads a word of the actual article.

2. It must tell what you are offering and the rights involved.
3. It must describe any additional items or services you can provide.
4. It must tell how the manuscript will reach that editor.
5. By far the least important, it might talk a bit about you and your credentials.

Let's look at each of these areas, then read a sample reprint cover letter, with specific comments about it.

The editor doesn't know you, already gets too much mail, and has too little time to waste on an unexpected and probably unpromising letter with an article also enclosed. So your first (and probably second) paragraph has to make the subject of the article jump off the page. It has to make the editor say, "Wow!" or, "I'd be a fool not to want to read this article," or, at the least, "Looks interesting. I'd better read that." This is where you show the editor you can write, discuss the topic on which you have focused your obvious talents and why (by inference or statement) that topic would find high favor with her readers. This gets the editor to pick up the article and read it through.

The next paragraph is short and falls after the point where you've stirred the editor's interest. It tells what you are offering and what rights are available. You must tell who bought the first rights, when the piece was in print and what rights you are selling. I usually get right to the point, since I don't want to dally here: "As you can see by the article attached, first rights were bought by (publication) and appeared in print on (date). I am offering second rights." (I could say reprint rights as well.)

In the following paragraph you will want to tell of other items beyond the words that you are also offering.

These could be photos. Since photos are almost always bought on a one-time rights basis, you can offer the photos the editor sees in the article or any of the rest that weren't bought. You can offer to send slides or prints for the editor's selection, if interested.

They could be line drawings, charts, graphs or any other artwork that either appears in the printed article or that you could prepare to add to the piece.

You could also offer a box or sidebar that you prepared but wasn't bought by the first editor—or one you could produce. (If the text exists, you might send it along with the copy of the article to expedite the sale and show the reprint editor precisely how it reads.)

Somewhere in the reprint cover letter you must tell the editor what format you will be sending the manuscript in. If you say nothing, the editor will assume that you expect the copy of the article to be retyped or scanned, neither exciting prospects. You enhance the reprint sale by offering either to send the original text double-spaced in manuscript form or on a computer disk, mailed or sent by e-mail. Electronic submission is by far the most appealing.

As for what to say about yourself, the article alone will speak volumes, and the quality of the reprint cover letter will probably fill in as many gaps as the editor needs. There are three areas you may wish to expand upon, if it isn't done in the bio slug with the article: (1) if you have many publishing credits, particularly in this field, (2) if you have a related book in print or are an acknowledged expert in the field and (3) if the work described in the article offers some element of original, unique knowledge or research. In other words, inject more biographical information only if that significantly increases the importance of the article or why the editor should use it. Otherwise, the editor knows the most important information already: that another editor thought your writing was good enough to buy and use. The rest the editor can probably deduce from reading the text. If not, supplement.

Finally, don't forget to include either an SASE or a self-addressed postcard for a reply. Otherwise you'll never know that the editor didn't want to buy your words for reuse.

The reprint cover letter is a sales letter, on one exciting page. A sample can be found on the following page. Spelling, punctuation, grammar all count. Make the topic come alive and shout to be used on the editor's pages. Keep the rest businesslike, forthright, easy to understand and compelling. It's a letter from one businessperson to another, one who has space to fill, another with space fillers to sell.

Modified reprints

What if an editor wants to use your article but insists upon changes? Fine. But is it a reprint or a rewrite? That probably depends upon how much change the editor wants and who will write it.

(Your Name)
(Your Address)
(City, State ZIP)
(Your Phone/Fax)
(Date)

(Editor's Name)
(Position, Publication)
(Address)
(City, State ZIP)

Dear _____ (Editor's Name):

It's almost impossible to imagine how far we have progressed in 100 years, particularly for those under 25 who have grown up with refrigeration, TV, cars, movies, malls and videos.

In 1896 the largest unmanned, heavier-than-air plane weighed 28 pounds and ran on steam! That was the year the first Ford was built, with two cylinders—anybody over 10 could beat it in a race. Movies had just appeared, sun bonnets cost a quarter (and just in time because radioactivity was also discovered), nobody knew what a zipper was or had set foot on the South Pole, but America's first pizzeria was open (three years before the first Pepsi)! Forget computers, Butt-head or football helmets.

As you can see by the copy attached, the first rights to "Was It a Hundred or a Thousand Years Ago?" were purchased by *Bright Idea Magazine* and appeared in print on March 30. Since it's highly unlikely that readers of *Ain't Kids Funny?* would have seen it in print, I am offering you second rights.

The four photos with the article are also available plus thirty more I can send for your review/selection. If interested, I could also create one of two sidebars that will tie the text even more closely to your readers: (1) what life was like for kids in 1896 or

(2) a more detailed look at what kids did instead of TV, cars and dating (as we know it now). If interested, I'd have to know which you'd prefer and the best length.

I can send the manuscript (and sidebar) simultaneously in print form and on a computer diskette (please indicate whether you use IBM/compatible or Macintosh and the software). The photos would be the old-fashioned way; I have no way to digitalize them yet.

I've been in print 1,600+ times, which my children will tell you is as hard to believe as that 28-pound steam-driven airplane carrying people more than a few feet. But both are true, plus 50 other marvels created, discovered or designed since McKinley swept the Republicans into power, as the article shows. Should we keep this alarming news to ourselves? Please let me know if you are interested, in the enclosed SASE.

Respectfully,

(Your Signature)

If the changes are major, treat it like a rewrite, which will be discussed next.

But sometimes an editor just wants to squeeze the piece a bit, dropping a few words here, an example later. Or use his own photo. He will make all of the changes.

No problem. You might ask to see the final copy before it is printed, to make sure the changes make sense.

Or the editor may want you to tie the topic to his locale, adding in a quote or two, some local examples or even a sidebar that offers local specifics. He wants to use the reprint as the core, with modifications by you.

The more the labor you put into it, the more you might want to negotiate the price. Find out what the editor intends to pay for the reprint, then try to get that increased to compensate you for the additional research and writing.

Rewrites

A rewrite, in the least complicated terms, is an article based on an earlier article and uses most or all of the first article's information. It is rewritten to create a different article that has its own sales life.

Let's say you write an article about training in long jumping for the Olympics. You follow the usual format: complete a feasibility study, query, receive a go-ahead, do the research, write the text and edit it. The article is printed. Then you find two other, smaller magazines that pay on publication that are interested in the same topic, so you send their editors a reprint cover letter, copy of the published article and a return postcard. One buys a reprint.

But why end there? Why not go back to that first article and see how you can reuse most or all of your research to create other solid, salable articles?

For example, why not an article for the high school athlete called "So You Want to Be in the Olympics?" From the original, you develop a long-range focus and training program for any athlete in any field, perhaps using long jumping as the example—or tying in several examples, including long jumping.

Or an article based on three or four athletes each from a different country showing the paths they followed to the Olympics, with tips from each for the reading hopeful. If all four are long jumpers, you have less research but probably less salability as well.

Or four U.S. Olympians from widely varying fields, including long jumping, to show their reflections on having competed: Was it worth the effort? What benefits have they received? In retrospect what would they do differently? What do they advise the readers thinking of following their Olympic paths?

By now the process is clear: Extract something from the original article and build on it for a subsequent article. The more you can use from your original research, the less time you need at the feasibility, querying and researching stages.

The trick is equally as obvious: You need a clearly different article, one that has its own angle or slant, reason for being, message and structure.

Rewrites need their own titles, leads, quotes and conclusions built around a different frame. You can use the same facts, quotes and anecdotes but in a different way and for a different purpose.

Once you've designed a different article, it must pass through the same selling phases we've described: the feasibility questions, the query, the go-ahead, the additional research, the new writing, the editing and publication in a different magazine.

Since rewrites have their own legal existence (see chapter ten, "Copyright and Other Rights—Including the Internet"), you can even sell reprints of rewrites. You can even rewrite rewrites, then sell reprints of rewrites of rewrites. That's just a name game. The editor buying a rewrite calls it an article, an original work created for that magazine and its readers. He doesn't want to know, and you don't want to reveal, that it's a spin-off of earlier research. Does it have its own legs? Does it stand on its own merits? If so, the term "rewrite" has sense only to you, as part of the developmental chronology and evolution of an idea put to print.

Further discussion of rewrites falls squarely under the general discussion about how you create and sell copy. Since a rewrite is based on an idea that already sold and comes from research that has passed the test of acceptability, it simply has an edge on the competing articles—if it is worth using in its own right.

A summary of reprints and rewrites

The difference is best seen from the rights perspective.

A reprint is an article sold on a first-rights basis that is being sold again (and again). The original buyer purchased the right to use that article on his pages first. Once used, the rights reverted to the writer. Following the protocol described, the writer then contacts other editors offering the resale of that original piece, on a reprint or second-rights, nonexclusive basis. The copy is the same or includes few changes.

A rewrite is a different article based on a previously written article and all the research that involved. It's a rewrite only in the mind of the writer. To the buyer it must be completely different from the work sold, since first rights to those words have already been purchased and it is not being marketed as second or reprints rights.

Reprints and rewrites require attention to publishing proprieties. If they are done improperly, you can lose more goodwill, and future earnings, than you earn at the outset. The most important element of those proprieties is honesty—defining in your own mind whether the piece is a reprint or it is a rewrite.

If in doubt, discuss it with the interested editors. They don't bite; they just hold their purse strings tightly.

There's something even better than reprints or rewrites. It's called topic-spoking. Read on.

CHAPTER THIRTEEN

Topic-Spoking

I t's such a financial loss to fully research a topic, then stop after selling one article. With a modest turn of the angle or twist of the slant, almost any subject can be reworked quickly and smoothly into a second article for a similar market, and that into a third. Extend that logic to its fullest and you have topic-spoking.

Visually, that means you put the topic in the center and from it you extend spokes (like N-S/E-W direction arrows on a map or spokes on a bicycle tire, but as many as needed), each spoke representing another article use of that core topic.

Practically, it says that you find a topic from which you want to develop many articles. You set aside a certain number of research hours to establish a fact base for all of the articles suggested by your research, then you pursue each of them at will. The advantages? The time and energy spent creating each successive article proportionately diminishes while the income remains roughly the same. You become an expert on a subject you can return to for years. And very often the accumulated knowledge lends itself well to one or several books, with before and after articles becoming additional profit stops.

Alas, no writer begins by topic-spoking. (I didn't even know about it until I started doing it. Then I had to give it a name. You may call it by another name if you don't like mine.) Most newcomers find or create one idea, feasibility test it, query, receive a go-ahead reply, study the target market carefully, write a selling article and move on to another idea, and another, and another.

That may be the best route for true beginners, to learn the selling process fully. It may be the only workable approach for those with a barn full of ideas, raging curiosity, boundless energy, lots of time and little need for money. It certainly will be the best route for those who want to write and sell one article, period.

But for those with greater writing ambition and commitment, there comes a point when the enchantment of daily blazing new trails dims, or one of the key elements—ideas, curiosity, energy, time and money—becomes less abundant, and they ask themselves, "Couldn't I squeeze two articles out of this idea since I'm already doing the feasibility research?"

My counter question is, "If two, why not five? If five, why not a dozen? And if you're going to dig twelve articles deep, why not sell the resulting knowledge by other writing and speaking means as well?" (Let's call the selling by other means "3-D Topic-Spoking" and discuss it in the next chapter.)

Also, why quit with a $350 sale when, with progressively less time investment and effort, you could earn $3,500 or $35,000 from that same topic?

Where does topic-spoking work best?

If you wish to convert one idea into many articles, the idea has to be sufficiently broad to be approached from many slants or angles.

It must be an idea, or theme, that touches others' reading interest. A topic-spoking idea must have enough grit to compel potential readers to yank the magazine from the stands (after they see the article's title on the cover), thumb briskly through its pages to find your words, devour the opening paragraphs of that coveted prose and rush to the checker, cash in hand.

The best ideas to sell repeatedly are those which provoke almost limitless curiosity, anger, fear, joy, pathos.

"Cats" (or any pet) will work; "Caring for One-Eyed Siamese Strays" is, at best, one article deep. "Loneliness" can be a lifetime moneymaker; "Taking Care of Lucy Lemaille Larkstone" will be of passing interest to a very few, once.

So topic-spoking starts with one idea or theme broad and strong enough to carry a dozen offspring. You must have some passion for that idea too since you must do the extra research and write that selling copy a dozen different ways. Choose carefully.

A major difference at the outset

The biggest difference between a single article and one with multiple selling possibilities occurs at the research stage of the feasibility study.

If you're writing just one article from an idea, you follow the standard path: double-test it with a feasibility study, query, receive a go-ahead reply, study the target market carefully and write a selling article.

When you topic-spoke it, the research part of the feasibility study becomes grossly exaggerated. Instead of an hour or two gathering enough material for a solid query letter and assuring yourself that if the editor responds affirmatively you can provide what you promise, you might spend 10, 15 even 30 (or more) hours researching the theme in depth.

That is where the term "topic-spoking" originated, as this diagram shows:

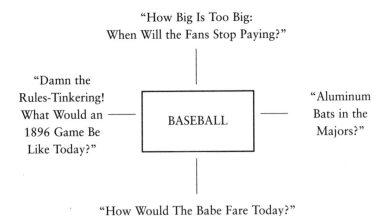

The center square represents the information gathered (or known) about the topic. Its size and depth directly reflect the amount of information collected during the research (as well as known or previously learned) before the first query letter is written. It is the information core of all articles to come from that broad topic.

That square will continue to expand, of course, as more articles are written and more specific information is gathered for them—or you simply learn more about the topic on your own.

The spokes represent the article topics. If the general theme is baseball, one spoke might be for "How Big Is Too Big: When Will the Fans Stop Paying?" A second might be, "Aluminum Bats in the Majors?" A third, "How Would The Babe Fare Today?" And a fourth, "Damn the Rules-Tinkering! What Would an 1876 Game Be Like Today?"

The baseball spokes are very broad. Almost any article about baseball could come from the central pool.

Some prefer the theme to be far more limited. If it were bass fishing, the spokes might represent bass fishing in (1) the Pacific Ocean, (2) Lake Nancy, (3) Highland Pond and (4) the Upper Marlboro River.

Whether broad or limited, filling that center is the major task and biggest risk the topic-spoker initially faces.

It's risky because gathering usable information takes time and there is no guarantee that the time spent will result in income received. A large, well-stocked information pool is no assurance that any editor will nibble on the resulting query bait. On the other hand, that pool makes it possible for you later to have a score of different, exciting lines out at once, to catch many and big fish simultaneously.

A five-pad process for gathering information

The feasibility study for single articles is quick and the information-gathering is usually informal, at least for the beginners: assorted notes on a few sheets of paper from which they pluck three or four paragraphs of poignant prose for their queries.

But you can't afford that luxury in topic-spoking, nor do you want to. (In fact, you can't really afford it for the single article either, as professionals soon learn. They quickly adapt something similar to what follows for every article idea.)

You want to be able to access every fact—where it came from and how to return to its source again—whenever you need it, now or twenty years hence.

Thus you need a system of collection and cross-reference, plus a place where you can note ideas for other articles, products or uses that occur while you are gathering the source material.

One suggestion is the five-pad process, with each pad representing a pad of paper on which a different kind of information is recorded. (This compilation could also be done by computer or on 3" × 5" index cards kept in separate boxes. Create a means of recording that works best for you.)

On the first pad, marked "FACTS," you would write down the facts that you find and might want to use in future articles. You may need several pads by the time you have exhausted the topic—or it has exhausted you.

The second pad is titled "REFERENCES." On it you would note where the facts came from, if the source was written.

The third pad, "RESOURCES," would be used when the facts came from an oral source.

The fourth pad, "EXPERT BIOGRAPHICAL INFORMATION," allows you to keep track of those fact-providers—usually authors of the articles you are citing or experts you interview—for two purposes: for biographical reference or for later contact.

And on the fifth pad, "RELATED SALES," you might note ideas for other articles, products or uses that occur while you are gathering the source material. If you limit yourself to article writing, you might call this pad "POTENTIAL ARTICLES."

Let's look at each of the five pads more closely.

Facts

On this pad facts are gathered for use in future articles.

Not every fact about the topic, just those you feel necessary to keep at your beck.

Each fact is preceded by a number, which is listed in order to facilitate cross-referencing where desired. Following each notation will be its source. Since the full information about each source will appear on either the REFERENCES or RESOURCES pad (as I'll soon explain), here it will be limited to a letter, several letters or a Roman numeral. The letter will be followed by the page number (and volume number, if from an assortment of similar books, like the *Encyclopaedia Britannica*).

For example, a notation about baseball might read this way:

1. Lou Boudreau broke his right ankle three times. A-140

The "1." means this is the first fact on the pad. After the number, you write the fact you want at ready reference. "A" indicates reference A; 140, the page number. At any time you could find that specific written source by turning to page 140 in reference A. If it read A-140 (VII), that would direct us to page 140 of volume VII in reference A.

A second reference—your initials—after the fact, thought, conjecture or notation indicates that you are the origin of that unique offering, though it might have been provoked or suggested by something else you read or heard. On my pad that would look like this:

7. More than being the only player-manager to win a world championship (Indians) as a manager the same season he was picked his own league's Most Valuable Player, Lou Boudreau added to that by being the only manager swapped for the team broadcaster; they changed places (Cubs). GB

Should the notation read:

31. "90% of the fans opposed trading Boudreau. They thought I was nuts." Bill Veeck (I)

that would indicate that the statement came from an oral resource that is explained in greater detail on the RESOURCES pad under (I), in parentheses to indicate that it is a Roman numeral, not to be confused with the letter I.

By doing this you can save yourself considerable time months or years later trying to find the printed or oral source of each notation.

How much information should you gather on this pad? On the one hand, you will want to accumulate every bit of useful information that you might need for future use. On the other, indiscriminate fact-gathering could lead to a dozen or a hundred pads. The problem is not knowing how many articles you will write or how broadly you may roam from your first intention. Two approaches can help.

One, if you have a clear vision of the articles you intend to write, jot down the titles or themes, the key reference words under which information will be sought and all the related subtopics that must be explored. Then gather solely those facts at the outset. Should other information encountered suggest possible future articles related to this theme, note the article idea(s) on the RELATED SALES pad. Also note the source of that information on either the REFERENCES or RESOURCES pad, with a cross-reference to the idea number on the RELATED SALES pad.

For example, the RELATED SALES pad might read, concerning a baseball article:

> #23. Explore future of designated hitter: retained in American League? Adapted in National League? Interleague play/Effect on AL team batting averages/Increased age of active players?

And on the REFERENCES pad, after the usual bibliographical information, it might say, in brackets:

> [also see pp. 12-15 for information about designated hitter, #23].

The second approach would be to start as narrowly as possible, focusing solely on one article and the minimum of basic information about the topic. That will expedite the preparation of that article and will let you test the topic to see if (1) you want to pursue it and (2) there is sufficient information to topic-spoke the theme. This approach sits somewhere between the more abbreviated one-article feasibility study and a grander expansion into a multiarticled topic. It's a rather cautious testing of the waters.

Another refinement might put like facts in closer proximity, rather than being scattered throughout the pad as they are encountered. You might subdivide the pages on your FACT pad, or use several pads, or even a three-ring notebook with dividers to collect your facts. In each subdivision the numbers might begin with a different 100-lot digit: 100-199 in one, 200-299 in the second and so on. Continuing the baseball example, the pad might be subdivided, and so labeled, by teams—Cubs, 100s; White Sox, 200s; Mariners, 300s, etc.—or positions or leagues or time periods, with the appropriate facts recorded in the proper locations. Presumably another subdivision would be "General Information" where those facts not easily consigned to the subdivisions could be noted.

Being from the old school, my mind envisions the notations being made by hand on legal pads or in expanded notebooks. But recording by computer has the additional benefit of allowing you, later, to be able to find, through word search, related ideas scattered throughout the pad, to be reassembled in a more organized fashion. Or simply to consign the facts at the outset in their own sections, folders, windows or files.

References

The immediate printed origin of each fact from a written source is noted on the REFERENCES pad, so one can later return to that publication to find the fact again.

If the fact in question is followed by "A-15" on the fact pad, source A is noted in full on the REFERENCES pad. A check on page 15 of this source will reveal the origin of the fact noted.

What kind of printed sources go on the REFERENCES pad? All of them: books, articles, reports, monographs, case studies, notes, diaries, law cases, telegrams, coded love notes or written material transmitted by computer. Anything conveyed in writing.

Standard bibliographical form is fine, with additional notations as required for the more esoteric sources, to help the future researcher retrace the source route.

When many libraries are used, or you wish to note the specific site location of material for later reference, it makes sense to follow the listing with that location, which I put in parentheses.

Finally, when the material cited comes from one source but originally appeared elsewhere, I note that too. How would I know that? Sometimes it is footnoted with its original (or an earlier) source; sometimes that is mentioned in the context from which the fact is extracted; sometimes one can deduce it from the information itself.

Here are examples of the suggestions just made.

A standard bibliographical listing, from a book: A-Einstein, Charles, ed., *The Third Fireside Book of Baseball*, NY: Simon and Schuster, 1968.

Another, a magazine article, with the physical location where I found that listing in parentheses. B-Nightengale, Bob, "Merry

Old Land of Oz Is Engulfed by Family Feud," *The Sporting News*, 7/1/96 (220:27,13, Santa Maria Library). If you subsequently find the same magazine in another location, add that to the site information inside the parentheses.

A third, a note, with both my source and the original source mentioned, plus the physical location where I found my source and the original source. C-Retold in a speech at the Elks Club by Elmer Abmer on 7/9/98 from Seymour, Harold, *Baseball: The Early Years*, NY: Oxford University Press, 1960 (Santa Maria Library).

Thus every time "A" is used it will mean that the fact is found in the source noted above after "A." The same for "B" and "C." Should there be additional information to include for a specific page reference or related to that particular fact, that would appear on the FACTS pad after the reference letter and page number.

For example, you might write, after the fact cited from B above:

"See REFERENCE J challenging the validity of this statement."

Resources

All facts coming from oral sources are cross-referenced to this pad. The fact itself appears on the FACTS pad; its source, in parentheses in Roman numerals both after the fact and on the RESOURCES pad, fully explained.

Oral sources in articles usually mean personal interviews between the writer and another person, who is usually cited in the text. The relevant facts or statements from that interview are included on the FACTS pad.

Inferences or deductions from interviews would be treated differently. They could appear on the FACTS pad, followed by the writer's initials and a reference to the source, like this:

17. Boudreau was the best known player-manager of this century but check the win-loss records and length of time managing of other P/Ms Frank Chance, Tris Speaker, Frank Frisch and Mickey Cochrane. GB [see (I)]

Or they might appear on the RELATED SALES (or POTENTIAL AR-TICLES) sheet as ideas or topics for further exploration, with additional annotations as needed. The example just cited, if it was fact #17 and also noted under RELATED SALES, might read:

> An article about past and potential future player-managers?—see fact #17, (I).

Other oral sources would include seminars, speeches, audio- or videocassettes, radio or TV presentations or any other forms of verbal communication.

How might a resource listing appear? Assuming I gleaned several facts from a TV show and this was resource (VI), it would be listed as follows:

> (VI) ESPN, 12/11/96, about 8:40 P.M., interview between Dan Patrick and Alf Timoli about the Miracle Pennant in Cleveland, Could it Happen Again?

Enough so that at any future point I know the origin of the fact that appears on the FACTS pad and is followed by (VI). Incidentally, all of the facts from the source will, likewise, be followed by (VI) on the FACTS pad. And I'll likely include the person interviewed by Patrick, Alf Timoli, on the EXPERT BIOGRAPHICAL INFORMATION pad, with any additional biographical data I can gather from that radio exchange.

Expert biographical information

On this pad you record biographical and contact information about key fact providers—usually authors of the articles you are citing or experts you interview—for two purposes: for biographical reference or for later contact.

You may wish to subdivide this pad alphabetically, A–Z, so you can quickly find the experts by letter when or if you need more information about them or wish to contact them.

Anybody knowledgeable about your topic qualifies as an expert here: people quoted in the references or referred to by other experts; authors of the key books and articles about your topic; speakers in the field; consultants; researchers; even lay journalists or others with special knowledge worth tapping.

Thus I use the term "expert" quite loosely. To me, in this case, it means anybody with solid information about the topic at hand, whether that be academic, experiential, by circumstance or even if someone has accumulated information from other experts.

I list a person the first time her expertise becomes known to me, and note any biographical information about her, including how I can contact her. Then if she appears repeatedly, I can continue to add new information to my database.

The library contains a wealth of biographical data sources, from the *Biography Index to Who's Who in* _____ to more specific, topic-linked references. Not only can I fill out a solid biographical listing on the sources I am particularly interested in, but new names will appear for my pad.

Employers, institutions and organizations often supply biographical fact sheets as well about their employees or representatives, which can be yours if you ask.

What do I do with the people listed on my pad? Usually I skim or read their books or articles for usable facts and ideas, or I directly interview them about my subject. The facts I then gather are kept on the FACTS pad and the source (if written) is noted on the REFERENCES pad or (if oral) on the RESOURCES pad.

Or I simply keep the name and bio information on reserve if one's specialty isn't my primary interest now but I may want to develop additional articles later on.

Related sales

On the fifth pad, RELATED SALES, you might note ideas for other articles, products or uses that occur while you are gathering the source material.

If you limit yourself to article writing, you might call this pad POTENTIAL ARTICLES.

Here is where you capture any idea that comes to mind about different ways the topic might be addressed.

You might think of thirty different articles you could write: some slight derivations of the article you are in fact preparing, some combinations of the different ideas, a simple update a few years hence and a few truly inspired or manic. From new slants, angles, twists and blendings come new sales.

The best time to snare these insights is as they occur, thus a pad to nail them down, in quick prose, for a more reasoned evaluation later.

This is also the place to record any other information dissemination ways by which you might share the topic beyond articles: A book? Several? Titles, slants? A seminar? A series of seminars? A speech or speeches? What about tapes: audio or video? Computer disks?

What kinds of products, beyond information dissemination means, does this topic suggest? How could they be integrated into the information formats?

Nothing is too bizarre for this pad. It's the doodle pad where all ideas, designs, brainstorms or just plain dumb, simple suggestions are welcomed.

Now that you've got the facts . . .

How does topic-spoking differ from more extensive research done before launching your queries? The selling process for each item doesn't differ. But the intensity of selling and the concentrated use of the same base data does require a different mind-set. For one thing, you may have fifteen solid article ideas on your POTENTIAL ARTICLES (or RELATED SALES) pad.

First, determine if they are best sold by magazine or newspaper, or if both, which would go first. Then prioritize the ideas since each needs its own development and special attention. Consider time factors (is the topic limited by geography and season—skiing in Aspen or Chile?), political considerations (a summary of all pro-candidates just elected and resolutions recently passed about raising federal highway park entrance fees), a "hot" topic that is directly related and so on.

Why not lump similar articles together to create a list of every available market for all of them, then determine which you'd approach first for each article, on the wise assumption that you'd limit yourself to one query per article and one query per magazine editor at a time? Musical queries.

And since you'd query widely on many similar articles, why not practice the same economy with your interviews? When you know you need one or two specific quotes for four different articles and the person being interviewed is a true expert with something to say for each, why not ask all of the questions while the person is talking?

The same applies to photos, if needed. It costs far more to return to a distant locale every time you grind out a new article or freshen up a reprint than it does to plan and photo comprehensively the first time you are there. How many rolls of extra film must you buy to cover a second air ticket?

The beauty of topic-spoking is evident. For twice or three times the initial research effort, you can sell ten to twenty times as many articles, mixing magazine, newspaper, originals, rewrites, reprints, black-and-white photos and slides.

This book has explained each process fully. In topic-spoking you plumb something you enjoy as deeply as you wish or can, then parcel out the information to as many editors as would buy it by as many of the means as you wish to use.

Pieces of the spoked pie

How might an actual topic-spoking look, if we look more closely at the pieces of the pie—or of the diagram we saw earlier?

One of the diagram topics was "How Big Is Too Big: When Will the Fans Stop Paying?" You might have sold an article built on that question to three (fictional) magazines, each article completely different. The first perhaps to *Cincinnati Magazine* about the Reds, in response to a sharp ticket increase and higher parking fees. The second to a Minnesota magazine about a hockey farm team charging as much as the top professional teams. And the third to *Sporting Weekly* about baseball in general, but using examples from other sports to provide a comprehensive view.

From that original sold in Cincinnati, a regional market, you might have sold three other rewrites, each focusing on another major league or Triple A team. From the *Sporting Weekly* article, sold nationally on a first-time rights basis, you might have sold a reprint (without a word of change) and one rewrite, the article as is but a long sidebar tying it to teams in, say, Seattle.

Then you might have reslanted the baseball angle and geared it to a newspaper preseason short, about 1,000 words long, that talked about changes leaguewide and nationwide regarding ticket costs, food, parking, concessions and any other fees—plus offered a tailored sidebar of 500–1,000 more words comparing that newspaper's local team's costs and policies with the rest of its league. And sold that four times, once as is and the other three with sidebars.

Do you see other possibilities using the same research, then adding to it to create distinct sales? How about a team that lowered prices? Where have fan numbers indeed decreased, and how much of that was linked to the team's "bigness"? Couldn't this topic be revved up every time any team in any sport significantly raised its costs? Would a study of the astronomical amounts of money paid to individuals and the effect that has on fan costs be salable? Could that be broken down by team or player or roster?

If we arbitrarily set a pay rate at $500 for a magazine original, $350 for a rewrite with sidebar and $300 for a magazine reprint, plus $250 for a newspaper article (add $50 for a sidebar), this slice of the pie or diagram might have earned you $4,800 in actual sales, plus opened the knowledge door to another $5,000 (or much more) in future pieces.

Once you had the concept down, knew the sources to tap for current numbers and had key people you could call for league statistics, all that would be missing for future sales would be a couple of phone calls and a quick review of the news sources regarding the most recent changes. If the first article cost you every penny you earned to get it right and learn the ropes, the last was 95 percent profit—and not a cent less accurate.

You could do the same with all four pieces of the pie simultaneously, and add a half-dozen more slices as the pie grows in proportion to your accumulating knowledge and insider contacts for interviews.

Aluminum bats in the majors? What about the minors? Problems using them in college? Earlier? Anything on the horizon besides aluminum? Any changes in wooden bats? What about the history of bats? Who used the longest? Heaviest? Shortest? Lightest? Any fatalities from broken bats? How often have they caught pros using fungo or leaded bats?

And since you're on such a profitable path, what about baseballs? How do they differ in the American and National leagues? Is the ball smaller in Japan? What's in that rubbing compound? Is the ball livelier this year (crank that one up every year and some editor will buy it). Describe how spitters, cut balls, sanded or roughened balls or any other mutilation affects the pitch—with the names of those known or suspected of throwing them. The fastest thrown ball? Slowest successful thrower? The potential article list is as long as your imagination. Write about uniforms, pieces of equipment, diamond abnormalities, trainers, night versus day ball. Then consider original articles, rewrites, reprints, magazines, newspapers, sidebars.

The thing that makes topic-spoking so profitable is the pool of knowledge you first create. It shouts ways that the material can be made to fit the needs and curiosity of almost any reader, and thus any editor. What makes that happen is your diligence in converting the shout into a sale. Or many, many sales.

CHAPTER FOURTEEN

3-D Topic-Spoking

W e've seen how one topic or concept can be the core of ten or a hundred related articles in all the buying media.

Guess what? You can leap out of the confines of the written word and sell that very same topic or concept by other means too. The best news is that a solid foundation in writing, with its precise articulation and need for a sensible structure, provides the best possible footing for sales in other formats.

A writer might pursue sales in any number of formats beyond articles and books, including audio- and videocassettes, talks, speeches, seminars, plays, music, dance.

You can use the same topic-spoking format as well. Instead of article ideas at the end of the spokes, put the means there and your mind to figuring out how that idea might look or sound in that new format. Some won't work; others will require a radical relooking at the idea to make it fit. And some are naturals. The topic-spoking diagram might appear like the sample on the next page. All that's missing is a topic in the center.

Let's take another of our baseball-related spokes and plug it into the middle. (Later, put your own topic there to see how it could be developed by other means.) What about "Damn the Rules-Tinkering! What Would an 1876 Game Be Like Today?"

If we took that literally, one could prepare cassettes and talks about

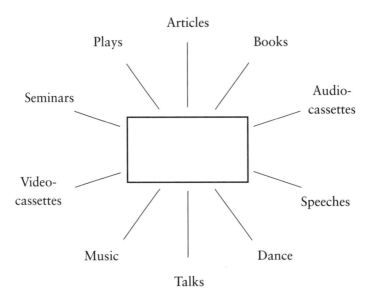

it, to show how things have changed by presenting a realistic rendition of a game as originally played some 125 years back, gloveless and with first-bounce pitching.

But if your mind wanders, as it's meant to do with this exercise, one could develop a dandy theme beyond the changes. It might emphasize that some of the basics never change—they are there for a good reason and deserve to be honored—but as society grows, it's proper to let its structures change too. Then baseball could be the example for both points, as it was in 1876 and how it is now, and why.

From that perspective, talks and speeches (even seminars) could be excellent media to address that new message to CEOs, club members, college audiences and anybody who would eagerly listen. It could be served up as well as a play or a musical or even the theme of some form of dance.

You get the idea. You write an article about how phonetics quickly reduce illiteracy, especially among the older immigrants. You could use all of the means to teach literacy phonetically. You could focus on phonetics to learn English for any particular language group, using examples in their tongue to demonstrate the sounds or show how they differ in English. You could speak to civic groups, PTAs, anybody interested in implementing literacy that way.

The purpose of this chapter is simply to suggest horizon expansion: Anything written can usually be reused, modified, expanded or markedly changed to be shared by one or many of the other means of communication. How that is done for each, and how you sell the product once created, is the province of other books, other than to reiterate that solid writing, clear organization and the purposeful articulation needed for success in writing vastly increase the chances of success in other media as well.

We spoke earlier, when talking about niche publishing, of empire-building by writing and speaking. 3-D topic-spoking is a tool to define the multimeans by which you can create your own empire, with one idea or concept at the core to be developed by the writing means we've addressed in this book as well as the other means of information dissemination suggested in this chapter.

INDEX